Shaping the Modern:
American Decorative Arts

at The Art Institute

of Chicago

1917-65

THE ART INSTITUTE OF CHICAGO *Museum Studies*

THE ART INSTITUTE OF CHICAGO *Museum Studies*

VOLUME 27, NO. 2

© 2001 by The Art Institute of Chicago
ISSN 0069–3235
ISBN 0–86559–187-3

Published semiannually by The Art Institute of Chicago, 111 South Michigan Avenue, Chicago, Illinois 60603–6110. Regular subscription rates: $20 for members of the Art Institute, $25 for other individuals, and $40 for institutions. Subscribers outside the U.S.A. should add $8 per year for postage. For more information, call (312) 443-3786 or consult our Web site at www.artic.edu/aic/books.

For individuals, single copies are $15 each. For institutions, all single copies are $19 each. For orders of single copies outside the U.S.A., please add $5 per copy. Back issues are available from The Art Institute of Chicago Museum Shop or from the Publications Department of the Art Institute at the address above.

Executive Director of Publications: Susan F. Rossen; Editor of *Museum Studies*: Gregory Nosan; Photo Editors: Karen Altschul and Jessica Kennedy; Designer: Jeffrey D. Wonderland; Production: Sarah E. Guernsey; Subscription and Circulation Manager: Bryan D. Miller.

Unless otherwise noted, all works in the Art Institute's collections were photographed by the Department of Imaging, Alan Newman, Executive Director.

Volume 27, no. 2, was typeset in Stempel Garamond and Solex by Z...Art & Graphics, Chicago; color separations were made by Professional Graphics, Inc., Rockford, Illinois. The issue was printed by Meridian Printing, East Greenwich, Rhode Island, and bound by Midwest Editions, Minneapolis, Minnesota.

On this page: George Nelson (American; 1908–1986). *Ball Clock,* 1949 (see p. 94).

Front cover: Russel Wright (American; 1904–1976). "Oceana" Box, 1935 (detail; see p. 59).

Back cover: Paul T. Frankl (American; born Austria; 1886–1958). Skyscraper Cabinet, c. 1958 (see p. 30); George Nelson. *Coconut Chair,* 1955 (detail; see p. 94).

This issue of *Museum Studies* was made possible by generous donations from Marilyn Karsten and Perry Herst, and Jay H. Dandy and Melissa F. Weber. Ongoing support for *Museum Studies* has been provided by a grant for scholarly catalogues and publications from The Andrew W. Mellon Foundation.

Contents

The Art Institute of Chicago

Museum Studies, VOLUME 27, NO. 2

Shaping the Modern: American Decorative Arts at The Art Institute of Chicago, 1917–65

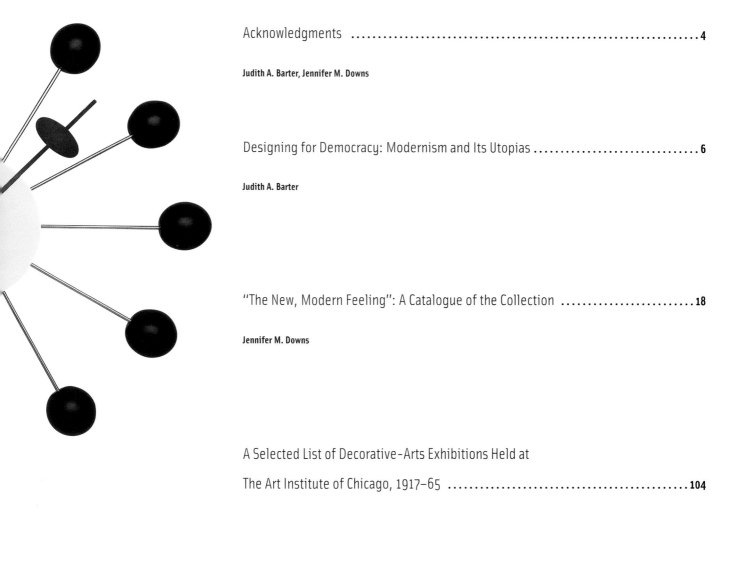

Acknowledgments

This issue of *Museum Studies, Shaping the Modern: American Decorative Arts at The Art Institute of Chicago, 1917–65*, came into being thanks to the interest and dedication of a number of individuals, both at The Art Institute of Chicago and beyond. James N. Wood, Director and President, supported the project from its inception. The generous financial assistance of Marilyn Karsten and Perry Herst—as well as their love of modern design—helped make this issue possible, and it is with our thanks that we dedicate it to the memory of their father, Perry Herst, Sr. Substantial support was also provided by Jay H. Dandy and Melissa F. Weber through the Orbit Fund. Both the American Arts Committee and the Antiquarian Society encouraged our efforts through acquisitions, special lectures, and consistent enthusiasm. In addition, the Community Associates of the Art Institute provided a grant to the Department of American Arts to further research the museum's collection of twentieth-century objects designed by women.

As the catalogue took shape, the Art Institute's expert Objects Conservation team—Emily Dunn, Barbara Hall, Tina March, and Suzanne Schnepp—worked to make every piece look its best, and answered a number of questions regarding construction, materials, and technique. Chris Fitzgerald, Preparator, Department of American Arts, tirelessly transported objects, with the help of the art-handling staff, for examination and photography. The photography itself was undertaken by the staff of the Imaging Department, under the direction of Alan C. Newman; many thanks go to Tiffany Calvert, Robert Hashimoto, Arawa McClendon, and Eva Panek for their help and perseverance.

Primary research formed the cornerstone of this issue's essays, and the staff members of the Art Institute's Ryerson and Burnham libraries were instrumental in making that work possible. Martha C. Neth secured interlibrary loans and suggested several sources, and Susan Perry coordinated the photography of period periodicals. The museum's own archives offered a wealth of information, and archivists Bart Ryckbosch, Deborah Webb, and Mary Woolever freely shared their time and knowledge.

Curatorial colleagues at the Art Institute were generous with their expertise and professional contacts, and offered thoughtful ideas and suggestions at every turn. In the Department of Textiles, we would like to thank Christa C. Mayer Thurman, the Christa C. Mayer Thurman Curator of Textiles; Sherry Huhn, former Assistant Curator; and Cynthia Cannon, Assistant to the Curator. Mark Pascale, Associate Curator of Prints and Drawings, and John Zukowsky, Curator of Architecture, also provided invaluable assistance. Andrew J. Walker, Associate Curator of American Arts, authored the Hunt Diederich catalogue entry (cat. no. 1), and offered wise counsel and kind assurance throughout the project. In the Department of American Arts, several individuals assisted in laying the groundwork for this publication: Suzanne Lampert, former Curatorial Documentation Assistant, and interns Mark Cunningham, Astrid Lavie, Mary Katherine Tierney, and Suzanne Villiger.

Other curators, scholars, dealers, and individuals offered their advice and expertise as well. We extend our gratitude to Avis Berman, Independent Art Historian, New York, N.Y.; Ashley Brown, Curator, Henry D. Green Center for the Study of the Decorative Arts, Georgia Museum of Art, Athens, Ga.; Mark Coir, Director of Archives, Cranbrook Educational Community, Bloomfield Hills, Mich.; Janis Conner and Joel Rosenkranz, Conner-Rosenkranz, Inc., New York, N.Y.; Ellen Denker, Independent Art Historian, Wilmington, Del.; Pat Kirkham, Professor, the Bard Graduate Center for Studies in the Decorative Arts, New York, N.Y.; Christopher Long, Assistant Professor for Architectural History and Theory, University of Texas at Austin; Graham Mancha, Design for Modern Living, London; Denise Marchand, Stuart Parr Gallery, New York, N.Y.; Warren McArthur III, MACs DESIGNs, Phoenix, Ariz.; Daniel Morris and Denis Gallion, Historical Design, Inc., New York, N.Y.; R. Craig Miller, Curator of Architecture, Design, and Graphics, Denver Art Museum; Steven Van Dyk, Librarian, Cooper-Hewitt National Design Museum, Smithsonian Institution, New York, N.Y.; and Andrew Van Styn, Applied Arts (1860–1968), Baltimore, Md.

It was in the Department of Publications that *Shaping the Modern* itself took shape, and we would like to thank Susan F. Rossen, Executive Director, for her support and adroit direction; Karen Altschul and Jessica Kennedy, who secured photography and photo rights; and Sarah Guernsey, who meticulously oversaw the production of the issue and shared her boundless enthusiasm for the subject matter. Our appreciation also goes to Jeff Wonderland of the Graphics Department, whose dynamic design for the publication captures the modern spirit of the objects represented.

Z...Art & Graphics, Chicago, typeset the publication and Professional Graphics, Inc., executed the color separations.

As a finished product, this publication would not have been possible without Gregory Nosan, the editor of *Museum Studies*, who consistently offered invaluable, strengthening suggestions, a fresh viewpoint, and calm, steadfast support. Greg's focused disposition and accomplished, intelligent editing helped to refine the text into a cohesive story of modern design. His hard work and dedication to this project are inestimable.

Judith A. Barter

Field-McCormick Curator of American Arts

Jennifer M. Downs

Andrew W. Mellon Research Assistant for American Decorative Arts

Modernist storefronts,
Chicago, Ill., c. 1925.

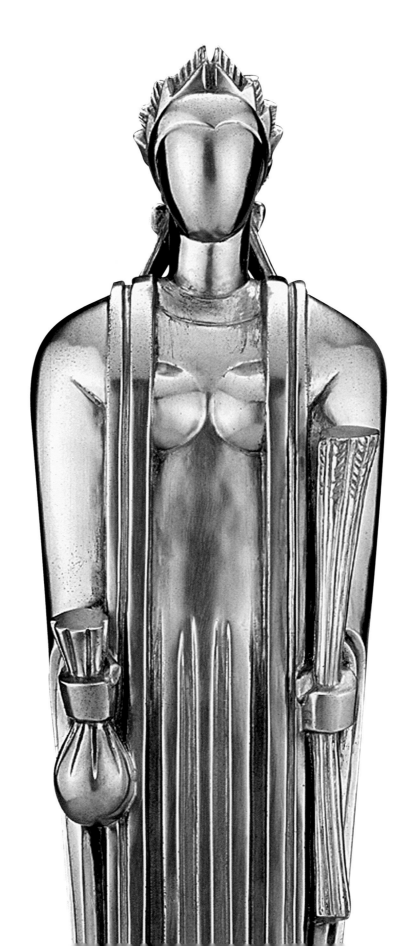

Designing for Democracy: Modernism and Its Utopias

Judith A. Barter

Field-McCormick Curator of American Arts

Let us therefore create a new guild of craftsmen without the class-distinctions that raise an arrogant barrier between craftsmen and artists! Let us desire, conceive, and create the new building of the future together. It will combine architecture, sculpture, and painting in a single form, and will one day rise toward the heavens from the hands of a million workers as the crystalline symbol of a new and coming faith.
Walter Gropius, 1919

Business is assuming the role of patron held by the church and aristocracy in past ages.
Frank Caspers, 1943

To construct a utopia is always an act of negation toward an existing reality, a desire to transform it.
Leszek Kolakowski, 1968[1]

There is no better way to introduce readers to The Art Institute of Chicago's growing collection of twentieth-century decorative arts than to offer a brief sense of both the ambition and complexity of the modernist movement, which dominated the cultural life of the last century, and whose practitioners sought to do no less than eliminate traditional distinctions between fine art and craft. As the above quotations suggest, moreover, they did so in a way that invested the objects they designed with a powerful, and indeed utopian, social importance. In reconsidering the history and diversity of modernist designs, it quickly becomes apparent that not all versions of modernism— or modernist visions of utopia—were the same, and that an aesthetic that began around the turn of the twentieth century with an eye toward socialist, democratic reform ended up, by midcentury, as the visual language of American consumer capitalism. Our story here is a tale of how a European-inflected style established and transformed itself on American soil—and on a local level in Chicago's museums, department stores, and expositions—sharing space with historicist designs, experimenting with American forms, and working its way into a central position in both the American marketplace and the national imagination.

Historical hindsight allows us to describe modernism as an extended revolution that emphasized new technologies, new styles, new patterns of social relations, and a new challenge to traditional forms of aesthetic thought. Modernism was far from uniform, however; as the social historian Raymond Williams famously explained, it was often more recognizable by what it was breaking away from than what it was moving toward.[2] It is perhaps more useful to think about modernism as a collection of related styles, dating from the 1890s to the 1950s, and including the Wiener Werkstätte, Deutscher Werkbund, De Stijl, German Bauhaus, French Art Moderne, Scandinavian organicist, and American streamlining schools. Such modernist approaches were characterized by rich variations that arose from differing national design traditions, and preferences for diverse materials and methods of manufacture.

While eighteenth- and nineteenth-century antiquarians valued art objects for their intrinsic worth and historical associations (such as

Figure 1

Frank Lloyd Wright
(American; 1867–1959).
Rendering of the
living room of the
Avery Coonley House,
Riverside, Ill. (1908).
*Ausgeführte Bauten
und Entwürfe von
Frank Lloyd Wright*
(Berlin, 1922), pl. 57.

their relationship to classical sources), modernist designers in general eschewed historicism and decoration, and aimed to achieve in their work a complete integration of art, science, and technology. For them the object, like the human being, ideally represented a balance of the emotional and the intellectual, the integration of art and life, and the acknowledgment of human need and potential in all things.[3] Highly influential was the notion of *Gesamtkunstwerk*, or the "total work of art," which blurs the lines between furniture, glass, pictures, sculpture, and their settings. Indeed, many leading modernists were at once architects, artists, and graphic and industrial designers who crossed traditional professional boundaries in order to create complete environments for living.

While modernism issued a clear call to reject history and celebrate the new, it did not, like Venus, rise full-grown from the sea. If it formed a clear break with the past, modernism drew from it as well—especially from the utopian vision of its immediate precursor,

the Arts and Crafts movement. Founded in the mid-nineteenth century by William Morris, John Ruskin, and other English intellectuals and socialists, the Arts and Crafts movement was itself decidedly antimodern, decrying the evils of industrialization, the loss of individual craftsmanship and dignity, and the shoddy products of machine manufacture. Turning nostalgically to a preindustrial model of life and labor, its proponents glorified the handwork of folk traditions and medieval guilds. They espoused the simple, "honest" crafting of objects that were devoid of any decoration which might obscure the simplicity of their materials and construction.[4]

Influential on the architecture and design of early modernists such as Frank Lloyd Wright in America (see fig. 1), the Arts and Crafts philosophy inspired European followers such as Charles Rennie Mackintosh in Glasgow and the Wiener Werkstätte in Vienna (see fig. 2), and remained popular well into the twentieth century; indeed, two of the earliest Arts and Crafts societies in the United States were founded in Boston and Chicago in 1897.[5] But the movement's emphasis on hand labor—and on quality materials that might bring particular pleasure to craftspeople—resulted in products that were simply too expensive for their intended audiences to afford, and undercut the socialist ideas of theorists such as Morris, who dreamed of satisfied, skilled workers producing fine, beautifully designed objects for every home. Summing up this dilemma, Morris himself complained: "I have got to understand thoroughly the manner of work under which the Art of the Middle Ages was done, and that is the only manner of work which can turn out popular art, only to discover that it is impossible to work in that manner in the profit-grinding society. . . ."[6] In practice, Morris's populist dream collided with the reality of capitalism.

While Arts and Crafts practitioners regarded the machine as the enemy, it was not long before a younger set of modernist designers began to find the look, materials, and use of the machine practical, alluring, and inspirational, and started to imagine the social potential of mass-produced decorative arts in a fundamentally different way. In the wake of World War I, which introduced tempered glass, tubular metals, and processed wood products into the marketplace, early modernist designers such as Marcel Breuer, Le Corbusier, Walter Gropius, and Ludwig Mies van der Rohe, among others, incorporated these industrial materials into their work. During the mid-1920s, for example, at the Bauhaus art school in Dessau, Germany, Breuer and Gropius created spare interiors decorated with austere, durable, lightweightmetal furniture of a standardized design (see fig. 3)—not unlike newly available appliances such as vacuum cleaners and refrigerators—and promoted their creations as affordable, hygienic, and resilient alternatives to traditional home furnishings.

While the forms of these designs were in part dictated by the materials of which they were made, many designers also preferred the machine-inspired look because they believed it allowed them to fashion a newer, simpler, and more affordable environment for the post–World War I world. Modernists took up the Arts and Crafts reformist program of producing holistically conceived, well-designed objects for everyday use, and embraced the philosophy that good design might, by bringing unity to the arts, operate as a tool for social change. Unlike Arts and Crafts adherents, however, modernists imagined that they might reach consumers more effectively by working with industry to create standardized, cheaply manufactured products. The machine, they thought, could help democratize design, and bring about a utopia characterized not by reviving the past, but by achieving technological advances that would result in a higher standard of living for all. Arts and Crafts antiquarianism and modernist futurism might at first seem to have existed in opposition to one another, but they were in fact

Figure 2

Josef Hoffmann (Austrian; 1870–1956). Dining room for the Palais Stoclet, Brussels (1905–11). Photo: Bildarchiv Photo Marburg.

Figure 3

Walter Gropius
(American, born
Germany; 1883–1969).
Dining room in
one of the "Master's
Houses," Bauhaus,
Dessau, Germany
(1925). Marcel Breuer
(American, born
Hungary; 1902–1981)
designed the tubular-
steel table and chairs,
and László Moholy-
Nagy (American, born
Hungary; 1895–1946)
conceived the wall and
ceiling painting.
Courtesy of the
Bauhaus-Archiv, Berlin.

its proponents, for example, were particularly inspired by late-eighteenth- and early-nineteenth-century French neoclassical furnishings.[8] Like other modernisms, Art Deco was informed by what came before it, and nineteenth-century French decorative arts were shaped by an exaltation of the ancien régime, of "those traditions, all French, of grace, refinement, of elegance, and, to be sure, of luxury."[9] Unlike other European modernists, whose social idealism lead them to unite in groups such as the Wiener Werkstätte, Bauhaus, and De Stijl, to design, produce, and distribute modern objects, many French practitioners still relied on a design concept based on the aristocratic and craft traditions of the eighteenth century.[10] Perhaps more importantly, the French continued to approach decoration as a separate issue, while by the 1920s other devotees of modernism in Austria, Germany, and Holland had come to treat it as part of an uncluttered, totally designed architectural environment.[11]

In America, however, the history, stakes, and social uses of modern design were substantially different. Emerging from an extended moment during which, as Herbert Hoover admitted self-consciously, the nation's designers "had almost nothing to exhibit in the modern spirit," Americans were presented with the challenge of forging a modern style of their own through both innovation and imitation (see pp. 19–21).[12] One direction of reaction is suggested by the designs of the Austrian immigrant Paul T. Frankl, who embraced the skyscraper as the signal motif in his own attempt to create a distinctively American brand of modernism (see cat. no. 5). To arrive at his vision of unadorned verticality, Frankl rejected historical models and fine materials—instead, he promoted the skyscraper as a compelling symbol of a modern American culture that

equally utopian. While one glorified hand labor, bejeweled coffers, and silver tankards, and the other promised the efficiency of manufactured chrome and glass, both believed in something more compelling than the present.[7]

Not all modernist styles, however, were fueled by a drive toward improving social conditions and making good design universally accessible. Indeed, French Art Moderne, one of the most influential statements in the emerging conversation about the shape of contemporary life and design, was devoted neither to rejecting stylistic precedents nor to embracing affordability for the masses. Popularized at the 1925 "Exposition internationale des arts décoratifs et industriels modernes" in Paris (see pp. 19–20), "Art Deco," as this style came to be called, was characterized by its designers' and consumers' persistent appetite for luxurious materials and historical references;

was driven and shaped by the forces of industry. The skyscraper represented a similar optimism in the work of contemporary artists such as Georgia O'Keeffe (see fig. 4) and John Bradley Storrs, whose gleaming figure *Ceres* (fig. 5), commissioned for the top of the Chicago Board of Trade Building (1927–30), epitomizes the connection between sleek modern design, progress, and the power of business that fascinated the American public for years to come.

Of the modernist styles, both European and homegrown, circulating in the United States during the 1910s and 1920s, Frankl's antihistorical model was by no means the most influential. Americans living in major urban centers would have encountered a variety of modern furnishings in museums, department stores, and world's fairs. In Chicago, for example, the Art Institute played an important role in promoting modernism as politically progressive and economically affordable. The museum hosted the traveling exhibition "German Applied Arts" (1912–13), which featured the products of the Deutscher Werkbund, an organization of designers, manufacturers, and museums that promoted new German design. This pioneering exhibition (see fig. 6) demonstrated the diverse range of modernist expressions, and showed that artists and architects could work with merchants and industrialists to produce affordable objects that improved public taste. All the pieces in the show were for sale, and while the Art Institute did not acquire any, Chicago collectors purchased one hundred and five objects. William M. R. French, the Art Institute's director at the time, remarked that "in Germany there seems to be no distinction between artist and craftsman . . . and that intelligent and sympathetic cooperation between artists and manufacturers has proved a conspicuous success."[13] Despite the popularity of this display in the cities where it was shown, World War I dampened American

Figure 4
Georgia O'Keeffe (American; 1887–1986). *The Shelton with Sunspots*, 1926. Oil on canvas; 123.2 x 76.8 cm (48 ½ x 30 ¼ in.). The Art Institute of Chicago, gift of Leigh B. Block, 1985.206.

Figure 5
John Bradley Storrs (American; 1885–1956). *Ceres*, 1928. Copper alloy plated with nickel, then chrome; 67.3 cm high on 12.7 x 15.2 cm base (26 ½ in. high on 5 x 6 base). The Art Institute of Chicago, gift of John N. Stern, 1981.538.

enthusiasm for things German, and further Werkbund exhibitions did not materialize. By 1922, however, objects from Joseph Urban's New-York based Wiener Werkstätte of America, Incorporated, prompted positive press when exhibited at the Art Institute (see fig. 7). One Chicago reviewer, for example, proclaimed that the new life and vitality he perceived in the show reflected an international movement that rejected conservatism and emerged from the work of "progressive leaders in present-day ideas who feel that in our times there must be progress and perpetual change in decorative arts even as there are in all the arts and sciences."[14]

The majority of modernist furnishings available to Chicagoans at this moment seem to have been offered for sale at high prices, and in relatively exclusive establishments. Like major retailers in other American cities, Chicago's department stores showed a great interest in Art Moderne (or Art Deco), and promoted it more aggressively than other modernist styles. Commercial interest in modern furnishings seems to have escalated after the 1927 "Swedish Contemporary Decorative Arts" exhibition at the Art Institute (see fig. 8), whose name reflected its organizers' goal of presenting to viewers the elegance traditionally associated with handblown glass, fine weavings, and other handcrafted goods, often at less expensive prices than French imports.[15] There was in fact an implicit assumption on the part of Chicagoans that Swedish society—and Scandinavian culture generally—was more democratic than the French, more like the comfortable lifestyle of the American middle class.[16]

At around the same time, the exclusive Charles A. Stevens and Brothers store, located in Chicago's Loop business district, also opened a small gift gallery (see fig. 9). At Stevens Brothers, modern furnishings took on a chic, sophisticated look, much like the store's expensive dresses. Catering to a wealthy clientele, the firm developed a design vision in keeping with the elegance and richness of French modernism. Stevens Brothers believed that modernist furniture should not be mass-produced of new industrial materials, but rather handcrafted of fine fabric, leather, and wood, as a testament to the discriminating taste of both designer and patron.[17] A different interpretation of the modernist aesthetic prevailed at another new establishment, Secession, Ltd., opened in 1927 by architects Robert Switzer and Harold Warner (see fig. 10). Influenced by their travels in Austria, France, Germany, and Sweden, Switzer and Warner decorated their shop's interior in blacks, whites, and grays, with unbleached muslin fabrics, German and Swedish wallpapers, and tall, black cabinets of their own design, not unlike Frankl's "skyscrapers."[18]

The Art Institute participated in the commercial promotion of modernist furnishings as well: In 1928 Warner, along with the museum's current director, Robert Harshe, joined a group of Chicago businessmen and arts organizations in sponsoring the "Exposition of Modern American Industrial and Decorative Arts," held at Mandel Brothers department store (see fig. 11). Although the organizers exhibited a copper coffee table and mirror by Frankl, the decorative accessories they displayed were mainly examples of French Art Deco design.[19] As at Stevens Brothers, the emphasis was not on the functionalism or economic restraint often associated with German modernist furnishings, but instead on the rare, luxurious materials that characterized the upscale Art Moderne style. In the wake of World War I, prosperous Chicagoans, traditionally francophilic in the first place, regarded expensive, chic Parisian designs more favorably than German ones.

Of all the Chicago department stores selling finer furnishings during the 1920s, only Marshall Field and Company catered to a wide range of tastes and budgets. Making the obvious connection between modernist design and expense, one critic wrote in 1927 that Field's displayed its modern interiors in the model rooms of a "cosmopolitan" city apartment, and showed affordable maple reproductions of early-American pieces in its "budget house," which featured rooms furnished for under $1800. In these displays, homey, small-patterned wallpapers, hooked rugs, and chintz

draperies complemented "late-Georgian" and "Adam-style" furniture.[20] Field's departed from prevailing Art Deco influences in furnishing the "cosmopolitan" pied-à-terre, presenting German-modernist inspired objects by Peter Behrens and Wolfgang Hoffmann (see cat. no. 13), and silk doorway hangings by the Wiener Werkstätte of America.[21]

Field's uneven mix of colonial and modernist furniture can be seen, in fact, to have resulted from—and indeed to have capitalized on—a larger competition between historicist and modernist impulses in the 1920s. On a local level, Chicago, as a city with a continual visual history dating to only after the Great Fire of 1871, manifested its cultural insecurity through an attraction to the colonial past of the East Coast. This penchant merged with a wider national interest in America's eighteenth-century culture, which was partly a conservative reaction to increasing immigration and the perceived dilution of the country's Anglo-Saxon racial stock. It later constituted a reassuring, backward-looking response to the hardships of the Great Depression. Nostalgia for what was believed to be America's golden age prompted businessmen such as Henry

Figure 9

The Art Moderne Shop in the Charles A. Stevens and Brothers Store, Chicago, Ill. Photo: *Good Furniture Magazine* 30, 2 (Feb. 1928), p. 72.

Ford and John D. Rockefeller, Jr., to promote a romantic view of the national past through such enterprises as Colonial Williamsburg in Virginia (1926) and Greenfield Village in Dearborn, Michigan (1929).

Even as affordable imitations of colonial furnishings offered their users tangible, comforting reminders of a simpler past, a new, uniquely American style of streamlined modernism emerged in the 1930s, luring buyers with images of future progress and prosperity, and reactivating modernism's utopian, populist potential in the service of American industry. Indeed, after the Depression began, many American designers rejected Art Deco's opulence but retained its sleek curvilinearity.[23] Streamlining proved the ultimate marketing tool for a stagnant economy: industry redesigned products of all kinds in order to stimulate consumption and restore public faith in corporate America as the prime source of national progress. By aligning itself with machine efficiency, aerodynamic design, and scientific innovation, industry worked to remake its image, casting itself as an economic savior capable of defeating the worst economic disaster in American history.

An early, spectacular example of the connection between streamlining, technological utopianism, and corporate image-making occurred at Chicago's "Century of Progress International Exposition" of 1933, which operated to some extent as an urban, modern alternative to establishments such as Colonial Williamsburg and Greenfield Village. Celebrating the ennobling forces of science and industry, the exposition marked the city's growth over one hundred years from a small village to a national center of commerce, culture, and transportation. The futuristic forms of the fair's buildings, interior furnishings, and consumer products embodied the speed of progress itself. During the exposition, for instance, corporate sponsors furnished model houses of various styles with tubular-metal furniture (see p. 48, fig. 1, and cat. no. 13); the Chrysler Corporation introduced its aerodynamic *Airflow* auto design; and the Chicago Burlington and Quincy Railroad unveiled the *Burlington Zephyr* engine, which astonished crowds with its gleaming, stainless-steel casing and sleek simplicity (see fig. 12).[23] The Depression assured the transfer of artistic patronage from wealthy individuals to corporate sponsors, and at the "Century of Progress" exhibition large corporations displayed their (and implicitly America's) technological prowess through brightly colored, vertically massed buildings and pavilions (see fig. 13). The fair cemented the association of modernism with a new, fast-paced lifestyle, emphasizing streamlined living, time-saving technologies, and a vision of an American culture in which the machine enabled a future of limitless progress and prosperity.

During the 1930s, America's premier cultural institutions continued to join with business in promoting modernism and defining its shape: in New York, for example, the Museum of Modern Art organized a series of enormously popular exhibitions that began in 1931 with "The International Style: Architecture since 1922." In 1934 director Alfred H. Barr, Jr., and architect/curator Philip Johnson collaborated on "The Machine Age," which showcased more than four hundred objects ranging from industrial products to home furnishings and appliances. Privileging a functionalist, minimalist aesthetic over French Art Deco, the show solidified the museum's longstanding alliance with the Bauhaus and International styles.

This link between the United States and the International Style was further strengthened by the large number of foreign designers fleeing Europe in advance of World War II. Breuer, Gropius, Mies, and László Moholy-Nagy all immigrated to the United States, the latter two resuming their careers in Chicago—Mies at the Armour Institute (eventually renamed the Illinois Institute of Technology), and Moholy at the New Bauhaus (later known as the Institute of Design). Graphic and industrial artists like Herbert Bayer and Egbert Jacobsen found work at Chicago companies such as the Container Corporation of America, where they used modernist typography and designs to signal a new corporate "look."[24] During World War II, the company's chairman, Walter Paepcke, discovered modernism's power to promote products and, more importantly, to construct the public image of the corporation itself; many others followed his lead, aligning their corporate identities with the defense of democratic creativity, culture, and individual freedom and initiative. In the postwar years, at headquarters from Chicago to New York and beyond, sleek chrome and glass International Style furnishings joined modernist graphic design and abstract art as the aesthetic language of corporate influence (see fig. 14).[25]

If modernism emerged as an expression of American democracy in the boardroom, it took on similar importance in the living room. While corporations preferred expensive modernist furnishings as symbols of their affluence

Above:

Figure 10

Secession, Ltd., Chicago, Ill. Photo: *Good Furniture Magazine* 30, 2 (Feb. 1928), p. 74.

Below:

Figure 11

A "Living Room Fireplace Group" from the "Exposition of Modern American Industrial and Decorative Arts," Mandel Brothers department store, Chicago, Ill., Oct. 1928. Photo: *Good Furniture Magazine* 31, 6 (Dec. 1928), p. 315.

Above:

Figure 12

The *Burlington Zephyr* of the Chicago Burlington and Quincy Railroad, shown with a streamlined Olson Rug Company truck, 1935. Hedrich-Blessing Archive, the Chicago Historical Society.

Below:

Figure 13

Edward H. Bennett (American, born England; 1874–1954); John Augur Holabird (American; 1886–1945); and Hubert Burnham (American; 1882–1968). Travel and Transport Building, "A Century of Progress International Exposition," Chicago, Ill., 1933.

and power, American consumers were offered cheaper alternatives for use at home. For example, Russel Wright (see cat. no. 16), a leading proponent of organic modernism, declared the movement toward mass-produced, inexpensive, and informal design to be "a truer expression of our Democratic ideals" than custom-made, historical furniture, and imagined that through it Americans might "develop a more honest way of living."[26] Indeed, after World War II, designers and manufacturers used materials and technologies developed or honed during wartime—molded fiberglass and plywood, synthetic glues, and plastics—to create stylish furnishings that were accessible and affordable in a way that most earlier modernist designs had never been. The work of George Nelson (see cat. no. 28), Charles and Ray Eames (see cat. no. 22), Paul McCobb, and other designers fit the lifestyles of young married couples who were busy educating themselves on the G.I. Bill and raising families in what would constitute the greatest population surge in American history. Affluence had returned: most Americans, in fact, defined themselves as "middle class" regardless of their income level, and with that identity came a heightened desire for domesticity and affluence, intensified in part by the insecurities and hardship of the war.[27] The mass migration out of cities and into new, suburban, single-family tract housing emphasized the need for new environments, new possessions, and a new start.

In the post–World War II period, then, modernist design—which emerged early in the century from an urge to remake the world by providing good design to the masses—became the language of American corporate power and a symbol of populist prosperity. Harnessed firmly to the American dreams of home ownership, consumerism, and democratic freedom, modernism's utopian promise came closest to being realized not in Europe but in the United States; not at the hands of Gropius's million socialist workers, but through the workings of the marketplace and the hopes and desires of countless consumers. Ironically, perhaps, it was only a modern, consumer society, aided by technological advances and machine manufacture, that could make William Morris's nostalgic dream of good design in every home even begin to come true.

Today, it is tempting to look back at the modernist movement—itself no longer "modern," but a closed historical episode—as a failed experiment, and to criticize its architecture and design as standardized and mechanized, impersonal and inhuman. We would do well to remember, however, that Morris and his Arts and Crafts colleagues leveled just such criticisms at the Victorian styles they railed and reacted against. As we have seen, modernism's beginnings were not impersonal at all, but sprang from a deeply humanist goal of integrating life and art fully, and making the pleasures of living with beautiful objects available to each and all, every day. To understand the importance of such hopes is to grasp the moral and aesthetic attraction of modernist designs to their original users, and restore to those designs some of the human meaning that time and circumstances have taken away. After all, as Morris himself said near the end of his life, worrying that his idealistic scheme had borne no fruit, "If others can see it as I have seen it, then it may be called a vision rather than a dream."[28]

Figure 14

Skidmore, Owings & Merrill. The Inland Steel Building, Chicago, Ill., 1958. View of interior corner office. Hedrich-Blessing Archive, the Chicago Historical Society.

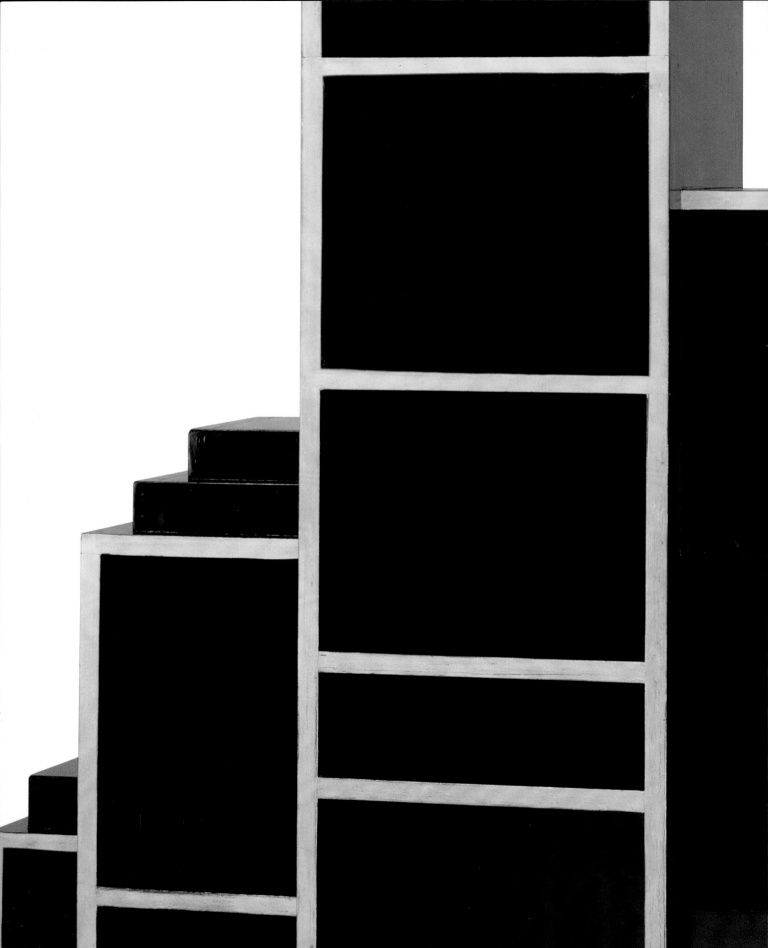

"The New Modern Feeling": A Catalogue of the Collection

Jennifer M. Downs

Andrew W. Mellon Research Assistant for American Decorative Arts

The Modern Spirit

The modern spirit, which is at present revolutionizing all the arts about us, has now broken through the last stronghold and has entered man's castle—his home.
Paul T. Frankl[1]

American decorative arts of the 1910s and 1920s were shaped by a wide variety of influences, originating both at home and abroad, which designers combined and transformed in their passionate search for a distinctly American vision of modernism. During the 1920s in particular, designers attempted to forge a modern style that embodied the country's innovative architecture, recent advancements in automobile and rail technology, jazz music and the motion picture industry, and the restless vitality of urban life in general. What emerged was a number of decorative forms that were by no means used in pure, consistent, or straightforward ways. These included zig-zags, stepped contours, Bauhaus-, Cubist-, and Wiener Werkstätte–inspired geometries, and neoclassical motifs executed in traditional materials such as wood and silver, and in a variety of innovative, man-made substances such as Bakelite®, Vitrolite®, and enameled metal. Designers hoped that these new creations would appeal to those who were ready to leave the past behind and embrace their own age, and, ultimately, the future.

In the late 1910s, a few Americans attempted to promote the cause of modern design, but achieved only limited success.[2] The onset of World War I, however, significantly decreased the numbers of imported goods, and may also have diminished the fledgling American interest in European modernist design. At just this moment, however, a number of Austrian, German, Hungarian, and Scandinavian designers— either stranded by the war's outbreak or looking for a new, vibrant cultural climate in which to work—began establishing careers and communities in America's urban centers. New York in particular attracted designers such as Paul T. Frankl (see cat. no. 5) and Ilonka Karasz (see cat. no. 10). Steeped in the progressive training that they received in their homelands, these émigrés were among the first to invigorate the state of modern American design.

Most Americans, however, clung firmly to the familiar Arts and Crafts aesthetic, as well as to the numerous historical-revival styles that flooded department and furniture stores, and were promoted through the work of prominent interior decorators such as Elsie de Wolfe.[3] The moribund state of national design was thrown into high relief in 1925, when the United States chose not to participate in the landmark "Exposition internationale des arts décoratifs et industriels modernes" in Paris because the exposition's rules specified that all works submitted should be modern, of "new inspiration and originality," and that "reproductions, imitations, and counterfeits of ancient styles" were prohibited.[4] This watershed event profoundly affected the American consciousness because designers, patrons, and critics were forced to acknowledge that even though the United States surpassed Europe in technological progress, it lagged behind in terms of design.

Although many were content to look to Europe for the latest fashions, the perceived lack of an American modernist vocabulary prompted a number of curious civilians, journalists, and designers, among them Donald Deskey (see cat. no. 7), Eugene Schoen (see cat. no. 6), and Kem Weber (see cat. no. 11), to travel to Paris to see the exposition for themselves. The show's impact upon these designers and others—who viewed objects such as French furniture, Swedish glass, and Danish silver, and measured international progress in decorative and industrial arts—is inestimable. Even more important, however, was the challenge that the exposition presented to American designers: to develop a definitively modern, recognizably American style worthy of their nation's scientific and cultural achievements.

Overall, the "Exposition internationale" invested modernist interiors with an air of elegance and luxury, and inspired the use of such terms as "Art Moderne," "modernistic," and, later, "Art Deco," which stemmed from the exposition's title itself. Apart from cutting-edge presentations such as the Swiss architect Le Corbusier's model of a standardized duplex apartment, called the "Pavillion de l'esprit nouveau," many displays featured geometric designs executed in vivid colors, and often incorporated neoclassical elements such as pilasters, frolicking nymphs, drapery swags, and flower baskets, and impressive forms with fluid lines and smooth, sleek surfaces.[5] Visitors were also struck by how French designers such as Paul Follot attended to decorative details in their model-room settings, which were in some ways reminiscent of earlier, integrated Viennese interiors seen in museum exhibitions, and in New York stores such as Joseph Urban's Wiener Werkstätte of America, Incorporated. Follot, like many French designers at the exhibition, employed luxurious and exotic woods; he also mimicked Cubist painting in his furnishings for a young man's room (fig. 1).

It was not long before American designers began to imitate what they saw in Paris, and at the traveling "International Exposition of Modern Decorative Arts," which visited a number of American museums, including the Art Institute, in 1926.[6] The American Association of Museums organized this display, which showcased selected objects from the Paris exposition in the hope of rejuvenating modern American design. Although Art Moderne examples inspired artists such as Schoen, American designers in general favored simpler lines and less luxurious materials than did their European counterparts; these stylistic choices allowed many of their pieces to be machine-made, and sold more affordably

Figure 1

Paul Follot (French; 1887–1941). Furnishings for a Young Man's Room, at the "Exposition des arts décoratifs et industriels modernes," Paris, 1925. Photo: *Good Furniture Magazine* 25, 4 (Oct. 1925), p. 189.

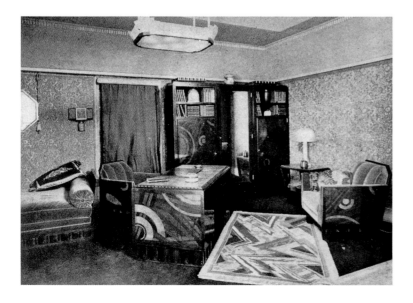

than expensive French or Viennese furnishings. Like the French objects which so often inspired them, however, such offerings were by no means easily accessible to many American consumers.

Other designers drew inspiration from contemporary fine-arts movements, particularly Cubism. Perhaps encouraged by the Cubist-inspired displays they would have seen at the Paris exposition (see fig. 1), modernists such as Deskey and Reuben Haley (see cat. no. 8) introduced Cubism's energetic spirit and fractured angles into their work, demonstrating their knowledge of European avant-garde painting and sculpture, and also linking their designs with the feeling of raptured aesthetic exploration often associated with jazz.[7] In sharp contrast, however, neoclassicism continued to remain a constant inspiration for many designers, and influenced many of the works shown at the Paris exposition. Like Erik Magnussen's graceful covered cup (cat. no. 3), neoclassically inspired pieces, with their restrained style, were capable of fitting into modern and traditional interiors alike.

The spare Bauhaus aesthetic also influenced the look of American decorative arts during the 1920s, albeit to a lesser degree. The tubular-steel furniture of Mies van der Rohe (see p. 49, fig. 2) and other Bauhaus-designed objects (see cat. no. 10, fig. 1) awakened the sensibilities of American artists such as Deskey and Karasz, who were inspired by the German emphasis on geometry, industrial metal materials, and, above all, function. Although some critics praised tubular-steel chairs as "the most logical furniture that has come out of extreme modernism,"[8] most Americans were unconvinced that such pieces could be used to create warm, comfortable interior environments. Even though many designers and consumers recognized the machine's ability to render well-conceived, reasonably priced

objects such as Gene Theobald's silverplated tea service (cat. no. 9), the Bauhaus aesthetic may have represented the idea of machine manufacture too forcefully for American taste. As a result, many designers themselves chose against using machines and man-made materials to realize their pieces, and adhered to handcraft traditions such as cabinetmaking (see cat. no. 6), silversmithing (see cat. no. 3), and studio pottery (see cat. no. 4).

Paul T. Frankl promoted what was perhaps the most individual take on modernism, one that strongly reflected the urban culture of 1920s America. He called for a modern style that was based neither on historical precedent nor on adaptations of European prototypes, but was drawn from the wealth of native, modern American innovations such as the skyscraper. This unorthodox approach sprang from Frankl's preference for extreme simplicity, and his idea that "things modern . . . have in them definite rhythm such as we find in modern dancing and music and in the frank accentuating of form in fashions."[9] In Frankl's optimistic opinion, which pervaded the ideas and creations of many American designers during the 1920s, modernity expressed itself both powerfully and poetically:

in the energy of the vertical thrust of towering buildings that push themselves through the crumbling red husks of the city of the past: in the speed of high-powered motors; in rapid transportation: in the Transatlantic liners; streamlined construction of motorboats, in airplanes and the flights of Colonel Lindbergh: in the general stripping for action, and the unimpeded release of youthful energy in sports and just now especially in the arts.[10]

1. **Henry Varnum Poor**

(American; 1888–1970)

Plate with Still Life, 1923

New City, New York

Glazed earthenware; diam. 21.3 x 3.6 cm
(8³/₈ x 1³/₈ in.)

Initialed on front: *HVP*; on back: impressed
Crowhouse mark

Logan Purchase Prize, 1923.354

Plate with Landscape, 1923

New City, New York

Glazed earthenware; diam. 22.6 x 3.6 cm
(8⁷/₈ x 1³/₈ in.)

Initialed on front: *HVP*; on back: impressed
Crowhouse mark

Logan Purchase Prize, 1923.355

These plates are among the the earliest examples of Henry Varnum Poor's painted ceramic wares, and received several awards at the Art Institute's "Twenty-First Annual Applied Arts Exhibition" in 1923.[1] Representative of his early painted ceramics, into which he typically incorporated figures, still-lifes, and plant and animal motifs, the Art Institute's plates not only reflect Poor's identity as an "artist turned craftsman," but also indicate his individual style, extolled at the time as "a more adequate expression of the spirit of today than that of our many contemporary potters."[2]

Trained as an artist in California, London, and Paris, Poor settled in New York City following World War I. Soon after of his first exhibition of oils and drawings in 1920, he began to explore ceramics at Crowhouse, a rustic studio that he built in New City, New York. He approached pottery as a new medium of expression, one that involved him in both the design and technical aspects of the creative process.[3] Indeed, like his contemporary Adelaide Alsop Robineau (see cat. no. 4), Poor's attention to every aspect of ceramic production was no doubt influenced by the work of Charles Fergus Binns and the American studio-ceramic movement. For the next decade, Poor created architectural tiles and ceramic tablewares, employing techniques such as the Persian method of painting or etching a design onto slip (liquid clay), and applying a glaze over it.[4]

During the 1920s, the term "modern art" was often used to encompass both fine and decorative arts, and it was not uncommon for painters and sculptors to design functional objects for domestic use (see, for example, cat. no. 2).[5] In 1924, critic Helen Comstock wrote that Poor's designs "have their source in the so-called 'modern' art, a phase in which Mr. Poor sees great possibilities for decoration."[6] Moreover, in the announcement for his first one-man exhibition to include ceramics, the artist remarked that the "natural development of modern art" was inextricably associated with objects created for everyday use: "Distortions, so disconcerting in an easel picture, have a sense of rightness when arrived at through the demands of proper space filling in decorative art."[7] Indeed, the concave surfaces of Poor's plates provide an illusion of depth that complements and enhances his painterly style of ceramic decoration, and furnishes a dynamic, tactile "canvas" on which he rendered his modern, abstracted scenes. Although the notion of decoratively painted ceramic plates was not a new one, Poor's combination of rustic earthenware with stylized scenes was extremely innovative.

In creating the Art Institute's plates, Poor used a speckled, off-white ground glaze, and applied thick, black circles to surround the central painted scenes, which he executed in shades of vibrant blue, green, and yellow, with violet-brown highlights. Poor punctuated these painted scenes with heavy, black lines reminiscent of German Expressionist paintings. In creating these decorations, Poor also drew upon his knowledge of Cubist still-life painting: he enhanced the flattened planes of the house in *Plate with Landscape*, for example, by applying a slightly skewed perspective, and placed the boldly rendered, angular bowl in *Plate with Still Life*—overflowing with subtly geometric bananas, pears, and pineapples—at an illogical spot at the corner of the table. Poor's plates represent an early example of Cubism's application to so-called decorative media, a practice that flourished during the 1920s in the decorative painting of Donald Deskey (see cat. no. 7), and in more sculptural manifestations such as Reuben Haley's "Ruba Rombic" line of glassware (see cat. no. 8).

2. William Hunt Diederich

(American, born Hungary; 1884–1953)

Dog and Deer Fire Screen, 1917/20

Made by the Art Metal and Iron Company,
New York, New York
Cut steel, wrought iron, and steel mesh;
85.1 x 113.7 cm (33½ x 44¾ in.)
Restricted gift of Marilyn Karsten in honor of her children: Lesley, Thomas, Jr., Liza, and Timothy Karsten, 1998.566

Working with sources that ranged from the mythic to the ordinary, the sculptor William Hunt Diederich consistently sought dynamic imagery, most often through compositions of animals engaged in combat or play. As he once wrote, "animals are a part of art themselves, they possess such glorious rhythm and spontaneity."[1] *Dog and Deer Fire Screen* represents this artist's achievement at its best. Against a finely wrought background of wire mesh, a cut-steel dog and deer are entwined in a circular dance of death. Their tails and fur are enlivened by jagged edges that not only add to the tension of their combat, but also provide the tabs needed to attach the silhouettes to the screen. As with sixteenth-century English firebacks, which experienced a revival in the 1920s, the effect of the blazing fire added to the drama of the scene depicted.[2]

Diederich was born into a privileged and cosmopolitan family in the Hungarian province of Szent-Got. By 1900, after his father's death, he left his homeland for Boston to live with his grandfather, the influential painter William Morris Hunt. In 1903, Hunt encouraged the young Diederich to enroll in classes at the Boston School of Art. Three years later, the young artist moved to Philadelphia to study at the Pennsylvania Academy of the Fine Arts, where he befriended Paul Manship (see cat. no. 17). After completing their studies at the academy in 1910, Diederich and Manship journeyed to Europe to further their training and begin building their reputations. Diederich studied briefly with the great *animalier* Emmanuel Fremiet and, in 1913, submitted his sculpture *Greyhounds* (1913; unlocated) to the Paris "Salon d'Atomne," where it was praised as "one of the finest, perhaps the finest" sculpture in the entire exhibition.[3]

By the time he returned to the United States seven years later, Diederich had firmly established himself as a decorative artist capable of working in a diverse range of media. In particular, he began exploring the possibilities of using wrought iron to fashion door-knockers, fire screens, and hanging brackets. When these designs first premiered in New York City in 1917, Guy Pène Du Bois, a prominent artist and critic, praised Diederich's metalwork and labeled him "a decorative revolutionist with one foot in the past and the other pointing a toe at the future."[4] *Dog and Deer Fire Screen* dates from this period, and represents a theme that Diederich had been exploring in other decorative articles, such as *Dog and Deer Lamp Bracket* (1917; unlocated) and *Dog and Antelope* (1920; unlocated), a fully three-dimensional tabletop sculpture.[5] The artist typically conceived his designs through dynamic pencil sketches, which he then delivered to craftsmen for manufacture. From 1917 throughout the 1920s, Diederich's designs, including the Art Institute's fire screen, were produced in New York by the Art Metal and Iron Company.[6]

The basic design of this piece is similar to that of an undulating wave, and gives the impression of continuous movement. The straight lines that comprise the two silhouetted animals exhibit a rhythmic flow that captures the viewer's attention. Throughout his career, but particularly during the 1920s and 1930s, it was Diederich's ability to render movement with deftness that captured the attention of critics and marked him as a "modern." As one journalist wrote on the artist's 1933 contribution to Chicago's "Century of Progress International Exposition," "Movement and rhythm, or rather, rhythmic movement has a particular fascination for him. . . . [For Diederich] a work of art is full of bounding life and vigor, and yet remains in exquisite balance."[7] In its abstract patterning and overall rhythmic design, *Dog and Deer Fire Screen* also resembles other modernist artwork of the 1920s, including the ceramics of Henry Varnum Poor (see cat. no. 1), who exhibited his work alongside Diederich's at the Art Institute's "Twenty-Third Annual Arts and Crafts Exhibition" in 1924.[8]

Part of Diederich's modernity, however, also depended on his respect for the past.[9] Although no precise historical source has yet been located for his fanciful fire screen, both its form and its animal-inspired subject matter bear a striking similarity to Slavic iron and copper andirons from the Middle Ages. In fact, Diederich's modern, kinetic ornament and his steadfast devotion to tradition became the dual strengths of his multifaceted decorative sculptures, and led Christian Brinton, the internationally renowned art critic and curator, to arrange the first major exhibition of his work in 1920 at New York's Kingore Galleries. Brinton, who had made his reputation promoting the positive aesthetic value of international modernism, celebrated Diederich's unconventionality. "For if modern painting has resolved itself into a struggle to simulate third dimensional effects," Brinton wrote, "sculpture with Diederich has renounced a certain rotundity of form, and has become light and lineal, an affair of rhythmic contour and expressive silhouette."[10]

More than likely, *Dog and Deer Fire Screen* debuted at the 1920 New York show, which propelled Diederich into the foremost rank of versatile modern decorative artists. During the 1924 Art Institute exhibition, for instance, Diederich received praise not only for his bronze doorstops and tabletop sculptures, but also for his cross-stitch-embroidery design of two fighting cocks (fig. 1). Since the mid-1940s, however, Diederich's career and significant achievements have fallen into obscurity.

For many years, modernist-derived injunctions against decoration have complicated both the aesthetic and historical reassessment of his diverse body of work. Only recently has Diederich's oeuvre, especially in the 1910s and 1920s, begun to receive renewed attention.[11] As with Poor and Manship, Diederich's stylistic freedoms signaled the emergence of a newly liberated figurative sculpture that, while rooted in the past, spoke to the twentieth century.

Figure 1
William Hunt Diederich (American, born Hungary; 1884–1953). *Black Rooster, Red Crest and Talons*, c. 1924. Cotton; 96.4 x 118 cm (38 x 46.2 in.). The Art Institute of Chicago, the Frank G. Logan Purchase Prize of the "Twenty-Third Annual Exhibition of Modern Decorative Arts" (1924), 1925.41. Photo: *The American Magazine of Art* 16, 3 (Mar. 1925), p. 141.

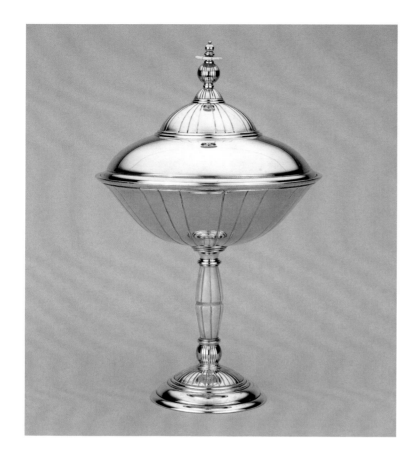

3. **Erik Magnussen**
(American, born Denmark; 1884–1961)

Covered Cup, 1926

Made by Gorham Manufacturing Company,
Providence, Rhode Island
Silver and ivory; 31.8 cm (12½ in.)
Gift of the Antiquarian Society, 1984.1172

In 1925, the Gorham Manufacturing Company—then producing predominantly
period-style and Colonial Revival sterling
wares—hired Erik Magnussen to design a
line of silver in the modern manner. In fact, it
was not uncommon for such companies to
retain well-known outside designers to balance their otherwise traditional offerings
with more contemporary pieces (see also cat.
no. 9). Unlike other designers, Magnussen
had complete freedom over his work, which
he oversaw from conception to execution.
Initially designing in a relatively subdued,
modern Danish idiom, he created wares for
Gorham that reflect the influence of his
famous contemporary, the Danish silversmith
Georg Jensen, who had been instrumental in
introducing modern Danish silversmithing
to American consumers. Often, these pieces
incorporate the stylized vegetal and foliate motifs favored by Jensen. A shallow
Magnussen bowl in the Art Institute's collection, for example, displays a scalloped rim decorated with cherry clusters and four diminutive "C"-scroll handles (fig. 1).

Even though the American public
embraced such designs, Magnussen acknowl-
edged a deliberate change in his style in 1926:
while retaining somewhat traditional forms,
he hoped to create "something very big of
America, and for America." The designer, who
felt that "America demands something plainer,
something vitally characteristic," aimed to create pared-down works that lacked the ornamentation of their Danish counterparts, and
stressed simplicity, function, and opulent materials. On a visit to Magnussen's studio in 1926, a
writer for *Good Furniture Magazine* testified

to his success: "It is not too much to say that he has developed an American style—a style that is plain, dignified, pure of line, and yet with an indefinable touch of the new, modern feeling."[1]

Although Magnussen's most severe departure from his more formal silver pieces was the controversial *Lights and Shadows of Manhattan* tea service of 1927 (cat. no. 8, fig. 1), he also made a series of elegant covered cups such as the Art Institute's. Less ornate than his earlier designs, and quite spare in form and proportion, these pieces not only employ the refined shapes and lavish materials so valued by Art Deco practitioners, but were also considered capable of fitting into "a Colonial background or into those pleasant mixtures of period motives [*sic*] that characterize the average American home quite as successfully as they could in a modern room designed by [Paul] Frankl [see cat. no. 5]."[2]

Indeed, the pared-down form and absence of applied decoration on the Art Institute's cup spring from Magnussen's ideas about the aesthetics of modern, functional silver: he felt that the decoration of an object should be secondary to utility, and in harmony with its form.[3] Although many modern designers in the 1920s rejected the revivalist styles that began in the nineteenth-century and have remained popular ever since, they often incorporated their knowledge of design history into their work. Perhaps as a response to the rise of abstract painting and sculpture, designers at this time, including Magnussen, found inspiration in the austerity of neoclassicism; the ivory finial, reeded stem, and restrained ornamentation on this piece are in keeping with the contemporary turn toward neoclassical taste.[4]

Magnussen left Gorham after only four years, ostensibly due to the poor sales of his modern pieces.[5] During the 1920s, most American consumers preferred the firm's historicist wares, perhaps because of the air of luxury often associated with traditional silver objects. Indeed, the company's chief designer, William C. Codman, wrote: "Recently a style so called 'Modern' has been introduced to the public, but it does not appear to have made much headway; and it only remains to be said that the fashion worthy of a place in succession to the best of the Georgian and Colonial periods has yet to be devised."[6]

4. **Adelaide Alsop Robineau**

(American; 1865–1929)

Vase, 1926

Syracuse, New York

Porcelain; h. 12.5 cm (4¹⁵/₁₆ in.)

Signed and dated on bottom: *AR* in circular monogram (excised); *1926* (incised)

Gift of Mr. and Mrs. Morris S. Weeden through the Antiquarian Society, 1999.294

The career of Adelaide Alsop Robineau, perhaps the most important American female ceramic artist of the twentieth century, was marked by her creation of a series of innovative porcelain forms, glazes, and carved designs. Created only three years before the artist's death, this diminutive vase incorporates the exquisite, crystalline glaze that Robineau perfected after years of experimentation. A technical tour de force, the vessel displays deep pools of silver-white crystals that cover its entire body, giving it a luminous, reflective appearance.

Like other distinguished women potters of her time, Robineau took part in the china-painting movement, which began in the 1870s and continued until after World War I. This national pastime provided an artistic outlet for amateur female painters, albeit a domestic one. Taught in local art schools, clubs, and decorative-arts societies such as Chicago's Atlan Ceramic Club, china-painters purchased ceramic blanks, or undecorated bodies, upon which they painted patterns that were frequently based on published images.[1] Such early experiences soon drew Robineau to more technical pursuits, including making her own clay and glazes at a time when most commercially made porcelain was characterized by historicist forms and ornate, painted ornament. Influenced by both seventeenth- and eighteenth-century Chinese porcelains, and by contemporary European designs such as those of the Sèvres artist Taxile Doat, Robineau often used published formulas for clay and glazes to create her own distinct pieces. At her Syracuse studio in 1905, she began carving and incising intricate floral, insect, and openwork designs into her hand-thrown porcelain bodies, and, for the first time, attempted the eggshell-thin porcelain that would challenge her for the remainder of her working life.[2] Around this time, she also participated in a summer ceramics program at Alfred University, in Alfred, New York, where she worked with Charles Fergus Binns, the founder of Alfred's School of Clayworking and the "father of American studio ceramics."[3] Binns spearheaded this Arts and Crafts–based studio movement, denouncing industrial methods and rejecting the idea of the traditional division of labor in favor of the artist's total control over every aspect of ceramic design and production (see fig. 1). Robineau was undoubtedly influenced by her teacher; like Binns and other studio potters, she created many works solely for aesthetic purposes, and viewed her work as a fine art rather than a useful one.

In 1910, she and her husband, Samuel E. Robineau, with whom she published the influential periodical *Keramic Studio*, moved to St. Louis, Missouri, to join a porcelain-making and educational facility established by Edward G. Lewis—and headed by Doat—with the goal of creating wares that equaled those of Sèvres and other European firms.[4] Here, Robineau executed the *Scarab Vase*

Figure 1

Charles Fergus Binns (American; 1857–1934). *Vase*, 1915. Stoneware; 23.2 cm (9⅛ in.). The Art Institute of Chicago, Atlan Ceramic Club Fund (1916.436).

Figure 2
Ceramics in the
"Eleventh Annual Arts
and Crafts Exhibition,"
The Art Institute of
Chicago, Oct. 1–23,
1912. The *Scarab Vase*
is visible at top center.
Archives, The Art
Institute of Chicago.

(1910; Syracuse; Everson Museum of Art), the most meticulously excised vessel of her career.[5] This widely celebrated piece, together with a Chinese-inspired lantern and other examples of her work, was exhibited at the "Eleventh Annual Arts and Crafts Exhibition" held at The Art Institute of Chicago in 1912 (see fig. 2). In 1911, however, Lewis's venture faltered financially, and the Robineaus returned to Syracuse, where Adelaide spent the rest of her career perfecting her carved and glazed wares.

Robineau most often applied her crystalline glaze—seen on the Art Institute's vase—to small vessels that were under five inches tall and intended for cabinet display. The jewel-like quality of the white crystals derives from the glaze's formula, which is low in alumina and high in zinc oxide and titanium oxide.[6] On an invoice for a similar vase, Robineau described the piece as a "Miniature round vase . . . covered with a fine crystalline glaze, in which the crystals have arranged themselves like a 'Swarm of Gnats' in concentric circular motion from any point of view."[7] Although this description also applies to the Art Institute's vase, each piece that incorporated this unpredictable, opalescent glaze is unique because the crystals formed as the glaze cooled. Less elaborate than Robineau's incised pieces, the Art Institute's miniature vessel suggests the aesthetic and technical advances that were changing the ceramics industry during the first quarter of the twentieth century. Like those of Binns and Henry Varnum Poor (see cat. no. 1), Robineau's experiments with form and glazes inspired a trend toward one-of-a-kind wares, paving the way for innovative potters later in the century, including Maija Grotell and Gertrud and Otto Natzler (see cat. no. 24).

5. **Paul T. Frankl**

(American, born Austria; 1886–1958)

Skyscraper Cabinet, c.1928

New York, New York
Painted wood; 213.4 x 83.8 x 40 cm
(84 x 33 x 15³/₄ in.)
Gift of the Antiquarian Society through
Mr. and Mrs. Thomas B. Hunter III and
Mr. and Mrs. Morris S. Weeden, 1998.567

Clock, c. 1928

Made by Warren Telechron Company,
Ashland, Massachusetts
Bakelite®, brush-burnished silver, chrome,
and enamel; 19.4 x 12.9 x 9.5 cm
(7⁵/₈ x 5¹/₁₆ x 3³/₄ in.)
Gift of Susan and Jerome Kahn through
the Antiquarian Society, 2000.129

In 1927, *Good Furniture Magazine* asserted that Paul T. Frankl was not only a modernist, but also "an original one, and he claims to have created, and hopes to develop, what he considers a distinctive American art movement."[1] By eschewing European historical precedents in favor of what he described as "continuity of line, contrasts in colour, [and] sharp contrasts in light and shadow created through definite and angular mouldings,"[2] Frankl drew inspiration from his surroundings. In particular, he championed the skyscraper as a source of a uniquely American modernist vision, both through his publications and in his own designs for home furnishings. While Frankl's furniture itself was a great influence on contemporary designers, in his prolific writings—most notably *New Dimensions: The Decorative Arts of Today in Words and Pictures* (1928), and *Form and Re-form: A Practical Handbook of Modern Interiors* (1930)—he ardently promoted a modern American style inspired by urban landscapes.

Trained as an architect in both Vienna and Berlin, Frankl immigrated to New York City in 1914; the outbreak of World War I during Frankl's travels in the United States and Japan prohibited him from returning to Austria. He established his own Manhattan gallery the same year, where he sold imported Japanese decorative objects, and began to design interiors.[3] As early as 1925, he created spare, geometric furniture that mimicks—quite literally—the setback contours that crown New York's skyscrapers.[4] Available in his gallery, these pieces were touted in *Good Furniture Magazine* as "the now somewhat celebrated sky-scraper type of furniture, which is as American and as New Yorkish as Fifth Avenue itself."[5] Frankl believed that the appearance, engineering innovations, and space-saving design of the skyscraper—a quintessentially American invention—expressed the modern

spirit of the times, and he marketed his compact cabinets, desks, and tables as appropriate for small, modern dwellings.[6] Indeed, the depth of Frankl's tall skyscraper pieces rarely exceeds one-and one-half feet; instead, as one contemporary put it, they rise "in a series of box forms to the ceiling . . . taking almost no room at all in a modern city apartment."[7]

The Art Institute's monumental cabinet epitomizes Frankl's designs. Its geometric form rests on a sharply molded base, and consists of a bottom cabinet section surmounted by a series of compartments and shelves arranged in a pyramidlike fashion, echoing the silhouettes of a city skyline. Smooth, unadorned surfaces exemplify the tenets of modernist design, and a black, lacquer-like finish is accented with dramatic silver detailing.[8] Although Frankl offered his skyscraper furniture in different woods and finishes, often painting the shelf interiors bright colors such as red or turquoise, he typically applied shimmering gold or silver paint to distinguish the shelves' edges.[9]

In addition to furniture, Frankl also designed and sold small objects like the Art Institute's clock, pieces that he meant to be placed strategically throughout the home in order to create unified, modern interiors. While Frankl featured this clock as an exemplary

Figure 1

Clayton Knight (American; 1891–1969). *Americana Print: Manhattan*, 1925. Made by Stehli Silks Corporation (New York, N.Y.). Printed silk; 62.9 x 64.1 cm (24¾ x 25¼ in.). New York, The Metropolitan Museum of Art, gift of Stehli Silks Corporation (27.150.3).

modern decorative object in *Form and Reform*, critic Helen Appleton Read praised it as affordable and "nontarnishable," qualities that were undoubtedly appealing to consumers. Read also claimed that the severity of the clock's design rendered it "unqualifiedly modern in spirit and execution."[10] Indeed, Frankl's clock relies exclusively on simple geometric shapes, smooth surfaces, and sleek materials, all of which characterize the Art Deco style. The rectangular, boxlike case rests within a stepped, black, Bakelite® base influenced by skyscraper forms, and includes enameled, blue-gray triangle and diamond shapes on the top and sides. Burnished silver panels radiate outward from the round face, echoing the silver edging on the skyscraper cabinet and giving the clock's face an illusion of depth. Although Frankl most likely intended it for display on a mantel, this timepiece—along with books and ceramics—may also have been placed on the stepped shelves of a skyscraper cabinet.

Primarily as a result of Frankl's crusade, both the angular setbacks of the skyscraper, and the wider urban landscape itself, emerged as prominent design motifs during the late 1920s, influencing, as Read suggested, "the decoration of every object from bookcases to handkerchiefs."[11] Contemporary painter and textile designer Clayton Knight, for example, included abstracted sections of skyscrapers in his *Americana Print: Manhattan* textile that he designed for Stehli Silks Corporation around 1925 (fig. 1). Skyscraper imagery, however, did not survive the Depression, which placed the monumental costs and capitalistic implications of the building type in perspective. Ironically, it was Frankl who in 1932 wrote: "The skyscraper, considered America's outstanding contribution to the present-day civilization, is but a passing fad. The tallest of them, the Empire State, is but the tombstone on the grave of the era that built it."[12]

6. Eugene Schoen

(American; 1880–1957)

Cabinet, 1928

Made by Schmieg, Hungate, and Kotzian,
New York, New York
Mahogany, rosewood, and maple;
114.3 x 100 x 47.7 cm (45 x 39 3/8 x 18 3/4 in.)
Incised on rear of base: *38586; S H K*
(within a circle); *6190*
Restricted gift of Fern and Manfred Steinfeld;
through prior bequest of Chester D. Tripp, 1988.448

One of few American-born designers to achieve critical success during the 1920s, architect and designer Eugene Schoen emphasized function, materials, and continuity of line in his furniture designs.[1] Although his furnishings have a distinctly modern presence—seen here in the sleek, simplified form of the Art Institute's cabinet—Schoen, unlike Paul T. Frankl (see cat. no. 5), intentionally incorporated both traditional cabinetmaking practices and European influences in his quest for a modern American style. In 1928, a critic for *Good Furniture Magazine* remarked that Schoen had "adapted to American tastes the best features of the French mode—the use of fine woods, beautiful inlays, sweeping, highly polished surfaces, and a practical utilization of each piece as a space saver in the modern *ménage*."[2] Part of a suite of furniture made for a New York City resident, the Art Institute's splendid cabinet reveals the way in which Schoen's vision of American modernism combined the stylistic influences of New York, Paris, and Vienna.[3] Perhaps because he catered to a wealthy clientele partial to luxurious French styles, Schoen did not draw upon his urban surroundings for inspiration, but rather looked to French furniture designers whose sumptuously veneered furniture and

costly, inlaid materials exemplified the Art Moderne style. However, Schoen did not employ traditional neoclassical motifs such as the flower basket, but rather looked to the strict geometric forms and patterns popularized by the Wiener Werkstätte (fig. 1).

A native of New York City, Schoen received an architecture degree from Columbia University in 1901, and subsequently traveled to Vienna, where he met Secessionist architects Otto Wagner and Josef Hoffmann, who was also a founder of the Wiener Werkstätte (see Barter, fig. 2).[4] Schoen established his own architecture practice in Manhattan in 1905, and in 1925 traveled to Paris to visit the "Exposition internationale des arts décoratifs et industriels

modernes."[5] Undoubtedly inspired by what he saw there, Schoen promptly added interior design services to his firm. Following Hoffmann's Arts and Crafts–influenced philosophy of *Gesamtkunstwerk*, which called for the total integration of a building's architecture with its interior and furnishings, Schoen soon began to display complete model-room settings that included his designs for decorative accessories, furniture, and lighting fixtures. In addition to presenting these interiors in his own showrooms, Schoen also participated in prominent exhibitions organized by department stores and arts organizations.[6]

Schoen's firm received commissions that included the interior designs for New York's

Rockefeller Center, as well as for banks, department stores, theaters, and numerous private residences.[7] Unlike contemporaries such as Donald Deskey and Kem Weber (see cat. nos. 7, 11), Schoen did not contract with large furniture companies to execute his designs. Instead, he worked closely with the renowned New York cabinetmaking firm of Schmieg, Hungate, and Kotzian, which also specialized in the manufacture of period-style furniture. Schoen also retained a level of exclusivity by limiting the scope of his work, promoting his designs as one-of-a-kind objects, and selling only to consumers and decorators, rather than to manufacturers or wholesale dealers.[8]

7. Donald Deskey

(American; 1894–1989)

Table, c. 1928

Made by Ypsilanti Reed Furniture Company,
Ionia, Michigan
Aluminum, enameled "Vitreo" metal top;
40.6 x 61 x 61 cm (16 x 24 x 24 in.)
2001.184

Although he is perhaps best known for designing the interiors of New York's Radio City Music Hall (1932), Donald Deskey was among the very first American designers to incorporate tubular- and strap-metal furniture into commercial and domestic interiors. In fact, the tubular-steel furniture that Bauhaus designers such as Marcel Breuer and Ludwig Mies van der Rohe (see Barter, fig. 3; p. 49, fig. 2) popularized in Europe was virtually unknown in the United States prior to Deskey's work.[1]

The dynamic design of the Art Institute's small table indicates Deskey's flair for abstract decorative flourishes, and also points to his early training as a painter at institutions such as the Ecole de la Grande Chaumière in Paris. In 1925 he attended the Paris exposition (see pp. 19–20), and the following year visited the Bauhaus in Dessau, Germany. Heavily influenced by both the rich materials he saw in Paris and by the functional metal furniture of the Bauhaus, he settled in New York and, like Paul Frankl (see cat. no. 5), dedicated himself to the search for a modern "American style." Deskey began his career in advertising (see fig. no. 1), but soon settled into work designing furniture, textiles, decorative accessories, and interior schemes. His early commissions included imaginative window displays for New York's Franklin Simon and Saks Fifth Avenue

department stores, and dramatic, hand-painted screens that he sold in Frankl's gallery.[2]

In 1927, Deskey joined forces with businessman Phillip Vollmer to form Deskey-Vollmer, Incorporated, which, until 1931, commissioned New York craftsmen to manufacture Deskey's designs for accessories, furniture, metal lighting fixtures, and screens. These works, in which Deskey married luxurious woods, chrome-plated metals, and synthetic materials such as Bakelite® (a plastic made from synthetic resin) led to several illustrious private commissions, including the Manhattan apartments of Saks Fifth Avenue President Adam Gimbel (1927), and the art collector Abby Aldrich Rockefeller (1929–30).[3] In these and other projects, Deskey pursued his intense interest in both sumptuous and industrial materials, which he combined in order to create a novel, distinctive approach to modern furnishings. Deskey's designs for the 1928 and 1929 American Designers' Gallery exhibitions (see cat. no. 10) also incorporated a mix of diverse media, and expressed his response to the spatial constraints of modern, urban living.[4]

Although Deskey had originally hoped to create mass-produced metal furniture similar to that of the Bauhaus, his designs for Deskey-Vollmer appeared in limited editions, and were therefore expensive. In an attempt to solve this problem and offer his designs to a wider public at a lower price, he contracted with major manufacturers such as Ypsilanti

Reed Furniture Company. For Ypsilanti, he created one of the first American groups of tubular-steel furniture, which featured lavish upholstery and Bakelite® accents.[5] Deskey also designed a line made from aluminum strapping, which included seating furniture, and tables such as the Art Institute's. This small piece was perhaps used as a cocktail table, and suggests the numerous influences at play in Deskey's work. In his elegant use of brushed aluminum in the base, Deskey responded to the example of functionalist German designs; the manner in which he overlapped the thin, ribbonlike pieces of bent aluminum, however, is characteristic of his own creative, decorative touch. Moreover, the designer added an unexpected, enameled-metal top that resembles painted or inlaid wood.[6]

In the Art Institute's table, Deskey also pursued his interest in Cubist painting. He shared this fascination with other contemporary designers, including Reuben Haley, whose "Ruba Rombic" glassware (cat. no. 8) offers its own, eccentric attempt to employ Cubist theories in three-dimensional forms. Like his early designs for advertising (see fig. 1), Deskey's decoration for the tabletop, which depicts a geometric, abstract vase of flowers, resembles the paintings of Georges Braque and Juan Gris, which he would have seen in Paris. By presenting his design on the tabletop's flat, canvaslike surface, Deskey may have tried to offer a more legitimate application of Cubist elements than those of his design colleagues. In 1933, for example, he recounted the various uses of "modernistic" motifs that followed the Paris exposition, and may have been referring to designs such as "Ruba Rombic" when he stated that: "Motifs were lifted bodily from all available sources and employed without regard for or understanding of their original intents."[7]

Deskey's metal-furniture designs of the late 1920s remained largely unpopular, perhaps due in part to the public's lack of enthusiasm for "cold and brutally hard" materials. Although a progressive group of designers and patrons considered metal furniture revolutionary, many Americans concurred with critic John Gloag's sentiment that "the designer may devise an interior in which chairs of shining aluminum are an essential part of the composition; but in such schemes human beings appear intrusive."[8] By creating pieces in concert with large manufacturers such as Ypsilanti, however, Deskey laid the groundwork for partnerships such as that of Wolfgang Hoffmann and the Howell Company (see cat. no. 13), who together, in the 1930s, were able to produce metal furniture that was affordable to a broad audience of American consumers.

Figure 1
Cover design for a Saks Fifth Avenue advertising brochure, c. 1927. Pen and black ink, black and gray wash, graphite on board; 35.2 x 27 cm (13⅞ x 10⅝ in.). Cooper-Hewitt National Design Museum, Smithsonian Institution, gift of Donald Deskey.

8. Reuben Haley

(American; 1872–1933)

"Ruba Rombic" Vase, 1928/32

Made by Consolidated Lamp and Glass Company,
Art Glassware Division, Coraopolis, Pennsylvania
Glass; 23.2 x 20.3 x 19.1 cm (9 1/8 x 8 x 7 1/2 in.)
Raymond W. Garbe Fund in honor of Carl A. Erikson;
Shirley and Anthony Sallas Fund, 2000.136

After it was introduced to the American public in 1928, the "Ruba Rombic" line of glass tableware—although derided by some critics as too bizarre for table use—was touted by others as "something entirely new in modern . . . glass . . . so ultra-smart that it is as new as tomorrow's newspaper."[1] Acclaimed for its highly inventive forms, "Ruba Rombic" is among the most original American glass designs of the twentieth century, embodying the frenetic spirit of the nation's cities in the 1920s, and capturing Cubism's dramatic angles and geometric planes.

A 1928 advertisement for Kaufmann's department store in Pittsburgh asserted that the pattern's unusual title stems from "rubaiy," a Persian word meaning "epic" or "poem," and "rombic," or "irregular in shape."[2] Some scholars have suggested, however, that the "Ruba" portion of the name refers to the line's designer, Reuben Haley.[3] Haley was a glass designer, metalworker, and sculptor who worked for a number of glass manufacturers before joining Consolidated Lamp and Glass Company, which produced a large and varied volume of colorful, European-influenced wares. Although he enjoyed a long and successful career, and was responsible for designs such as Consolidated's "Martelé" and "Catalonian" lines, the "Ruba Rombic" pattern is his most original creation.

Through the angular, segmented surfaces of "Ruba Rombic," Haley responded to the Cubist paintings and sculptures that artists such as Georges Braque and Pablo Picasso produced earlier in the century. At this moment, other designers were also translating energetic Cubist aesthetics into designs for functional objects (see cat. no. 7). In 1927, for example, silversmith Erik Magnussen (see cat. no. 3), designed a Cubist-inspired coffee service called *The Lights and Shadows of Manhattan* (fig. 1), in which triangular facets and contrasting shades of copper, gold, and silver lend a sculptural, almost whimsical quality to otherwise

Figure 1
Erik Magnussen. *The Lights and Shadows of Manhattan*, 1927. Photo: *Arts and Decoration* 28, 6 (Apr. 1928), p. 52.

Figure 2
W. C. Owen advertisement for "Ruba Rombic," *The Gift and Art Shop* (Feb. 1928), repr. in Jack D. Wilson, *Phoenix and Consolidated Art Glass* (Marietta, Oh., 1989), p. 46.

traditional forms. The Art Institute's "Ruba Rombic" vase is a rare, large, and particularly sculptural example of the pattern, which included tableware such as plates and cups, and novelty pieces such as candleholders, perfume bottles, and powder boxes. Offered in vibrant colors ranging from "Sunshine" to "Smoky Topaz"—the Art Institute's vase is "Jade Green"—the prismatic glass dramatically captures light and shade on its fractured surface.

Although designers such as Magnussen and Haley haphazardly borrowed Cubist forms exclusively for decorative purposes—ignoring the theories and intentions behind them—"Ruba Rombic" made an impact upon American design nonetheless. Even though Consolidated produced the pattern only between 1928 and 1932, it was successful enough to inspire imitators; around 1929, Haley was commissioned by Muncie Pottery Company of Muncie, Indiana, to interpret the line in

ceramics.[4] Consolidated also marketed and sold "Ruba Rombic" through retailers in major American cities, including W. C. Owen of Chicago (fig. 2). Announcements such as Owen's used bold graphics and dramatic sketches to portray "Ruba Rombic" as a new, exciting, and affordable "Epic in Modern Art," ideal for gift-giving.[5] A similar, 1928 advertisement for Ovington's bridal store in New York City observed that "even crystal has succumbed to modernism and allied himself with the prismatic and geometrical patterns of the age. The lovely ["Ruba Rombic"] service . . . scorns the conventional and in its daring departure from trite designs has found new ways to charm and beauty."[6]

9. Gene Theobald

(American; act. 1920s)

Three-Piece Tea Set with Tray, 1928

Made by Wilcox Silver Plate Company for
International Silver Company, Meriden, Connecticut
Silver-plated nickel silver and Bakelite®;
8.9 x 21.6 x 20.3 cm (3½ x 8½ x 8 in.)
Marked on underside: *Wilcox S. P. Co.*
(in an arch); *EPNS; INTERNATIONAL S. CO.*; 7036
Bannerman Foundation Fund; through prior
acquisition of Elizabeth R. Vaughan, 1999.680.1–4

Advertised as "at once classic and modern," Gene Theobald's innovative, three-piece tea service combines the traditional concept of a tea set with the clean lines, geometric shapes, and smooth surfaces associated with the Art Deco style, and at the same time suggests the machine aesthetic popularized in the 1930s.[1]

During the 1920s, improved automobile and rail transportation allowed prominent citizens to build suburban homes as their main residences while maintaining small city apartments. Apartment living for all economic classes, however, typically meant smaller rooms and little or no domestic help, creating the need for smaller objects that could be easily cleaned, and that were more appropriate for modern, space-conscious living.[2] Composed of a teapot, cream pitcher, and sugar bowl nestled snugly into a round tray, the Art Institute's service was undoubtedly intended for such a modern lifestyle: the compact ensemble was, according to the manufacturer's publicity, "ideal from the practical point of view for use in dinettes, breakfast nooks, on little tables, or for tea wagons. They [the pieces] are easy to care for and take up little space."[3]

Responding to an increasing demand for such objects, International Silver Company sought to develop modern lines of silver, silver

Figure 1

International Silver Company advertisement, *Vanity Fair* 32, 3 (May 1929), p. 113.

plate, and pewter holloware and flatware that it could affordably mass produce. Since the company had traditionally specialized in period-style objects, it hired outside designers, including Theobald, to create modern pieces such as the Art Institute's service.[4] Made by Wilcox Silver Plate, a subsidiary company, these architectonic sets were touted as "fine example[s] of what can be done in the ordinary run of production by an American commercial firm when it decides to appoint a modern designer of good judgement and sound taste."[5] Theobald's modern creations met with both corporate support and critical success: International Silver publicized Theobald as the tea sets' designer—a rare practice for large companies at the time—and actively marketed them to a wide range of consumers, since machine-produced silver plate was significantly more affordable than one-of-a-kind pieces crafted from sterling silver (see, for example, cat. no. 3).[6] In 1928, *Creative Art* praised Theobald even as it offered mild criticism of the modern-design climate in general: "With so much talk about

the mysteries of a certain kind of modern life we lead and our inspiration from machinery, or from peasants, or from skyscrapers, or whatever the designer's fancy happens to hit on, it is pleasant to see what can be done under rigidly realistic circumstances: a design to be made in a factory at a price that will get it sold."[7]

Not only did the manufacturer promote Theobald's mass-produced tea sets as affordable, but in a 1929 advertisement went so far as to praise them as "thoroughly in keeping with the fine old traditions of silversmithing"; they were also illustrated alongside a colonial-revival style tea service (fig. 1), perhaps in a similar attempt to associate these machine-made products with items seen as more hand-crafted, and thus render their modern style more palatable to consumers.[8] Although this piece was itself machine-made, it is important from a technical standpoint because angular elements, such as its three wedge-shaped components, did not easily lend themselves to machine production. In fact, the prototypes for Theobald's designs were reportedly finished by hand, and one critic wrote that "this design reminds the writer of hours spent in a small 'studio' shop trying by disparate handicraft to produce metal work that might look direct enough to have been inspired by a machine, and clean enough to have been made by one— in Modernism's name!"[9]

10. Ilonka Karasz

(American, born Hungary; 1896–1981)

Footed Bowls, c. 1928

Made by Paye and Baker Manufacturing
Company, North Attleboro, Massachusetts
Nickel-plated copper alloy; 4.5 x 7.3 cm
(1³⁄₄ x 2⁷⁄₈ in.)
Restricted gift of Mrs. Ann P. K. Frankenthal,
the Garden Club of Barrington, and the Lake Forest-
Lake Bluff Associates of The Woman's Board of The
Art Institute of Chicago, 1984.236–37

Like Gene Theobald's three-piece tea service (cat. no. 9), Ilonka Karasz's cone-shaped bowls—possibly used as salt-cellars—are reduced to simple, geometric forms that emphasize their function. Designed as part of a tableware line that included larger bowls, candlesticks, and flower holders, these small vessels not only demonstrate Karasz's fascination with modern materials and modes of manufacture, but also reveal her keen interest in both the aesthetic and philosophical principles of the German Bauhaus, which encouraged the use of industrial materials and smooth, undecorated forms.[1] While Karasz's artistic career flourished in the United States, she did not reject the influence of contemporary European design, as did contemporaries such as Paul T. Frankl (see cat. no. 5). These bowls, for example, recall the work of Bauhaus student Marianne Brandt. A teapot designed by Brandt in 1924 (fig. 1) features cross-supports comparable to those on the Art Institute's bowls, and the bodies of both are composed of geometric shapes that each serve a particular function rather than acting solely as decoration. Despite such outside influences, however, Karasz was celebrated for her distinct and personal "ability . . . to comprehend the innate quality of the medium for which she may be designing," and for her "individual style . . . always straightforward and sincere in conception, without any attempt at affectation."[2]

An extremely versatile artist, Karasz executed modern designs not only in metalwork, but in ceramics, furniture, graphics, textiles, and wallpaper as well.[3] One of the first women to be admitted to the Royal School of Arts and Crafts in Budapest, where the design curriculum was influenced by Austrian design movements such as the Wiener Werkstätte, Karasz, like many European designers of her generation, immigrated to New York, where she quickly established herself in the modern-art community of Greenwich Village. During the 1920s, she participated in a number of exhibitions that showcased her interiors and decorative arts, including the "Twenty-Third Annual Arts and Crafts Exhibition" at The Art Institute of Chicago in 1924–25,[4] and R. H. Macy and Company's "International Exposition of Art in Industry" (1928). For the latter exhibition, she contributed furniture, pillows, and wall decoration for William Lescaze's "Penthouse Studio" display.[5] In 1928 and 1929, she participated in the first and second American Designers' Gallery exhibitions, which

Figure 1

Marianne Brandt
(German; 1893–1983).
Teapot, 1924. Brass,
ebony, and silver;
h. 7.5 cm (2¹⁵⁄₁₆ in.)
diam. 15.5 cm (6⅛ in.).
New York, the Museum
of Modern Art,
Phyllis B. Lambert Fund.

Figure 2

Ilonka Karasz (Ameri-
can, born Hungary;
1896–1981). Dining-
room suite from
the Second American
Designers' Gallery
exhibition, New York,
N.Y., Mar. 1929. Photo:
*Good Furniture
Magazine* 32, 5 (May
1929), pp. 229–34.
On the sideboard at left
rests a vessel similar
to the Art Institute's
footed bowls (cat.
no. 10).

promoted American-designed modern objects
and interiors, and included the work of artists
such as Donald Deskey, Henry Varnum Poor,
Wolfgang Hoffmann, and Joseph Urban (see
cat. nos. 7, 1, 13, and pp. 12 and 53, respectively).[6] For the 1928 exhibit, Karasz designed
and furnished a complete nursery and a studio
apartment.[7] To the second, she contributed a
dining room that included a bird's-eye-maple
table and chairs, copper-colored mirrors, and a
few accessories, including a vessel placed upon
the sideboard that, although larger in size, has
the same form as the Art Institute's bowls (see
fig. 2).[8] Karasz was the only female designer to
complete a room in the exhibit, and her dining
room was admired as "uncluttered by detail
and reduced to the prime necessities of living
without sacrificing the air of comfort."[9]

Held only a few months before the 1929
stock-market crash, the second American
Designers' Gallery show sprang from its organizers' intention to "arrange an exhibition of
modern interiors whose cost would not be
prohibitive," and to feature objects that "have
been designed with a view to large scale production and made under the conditions prevailing today in machine industry."[10] On the
eve of, and during the Depression, plated metal
pieces with a contemporary look were aggressively marketed as affordable, easy to care for,
and suitable for both modern and traditional
interiors alike.[11] Indeed, Karasz's ultra-simpli-
fied design for nickel-plated bowls lent itself
to machine production and provided a relatively inexpensive alternative to handmade silver objects.

11. Kem Weber

(American, born Germany; 1889–1963)

Armchair, 1928/29

Made by Grand Rapids Chair Company,
Grand Rapids, Michigan
Painted wood and original leather upholstery;
102.9 x 54.6 x 50.7 cm (40½ x 21½ x 20 in.)
Mr. and Mrs. Manfred Steinfeld Fund, 1985.6

Serving Table, 1928/29

Made by Grand Rapids Chair Company,
Grand Rapids, Michigan
Painted wood, silver leaf, and walnut;
76.2 x 91.4 x 41.9 cm (30 x 36 x 16½ in.)
Mr. and Mrs. Manfred Steinfeld Fund, 1985.5

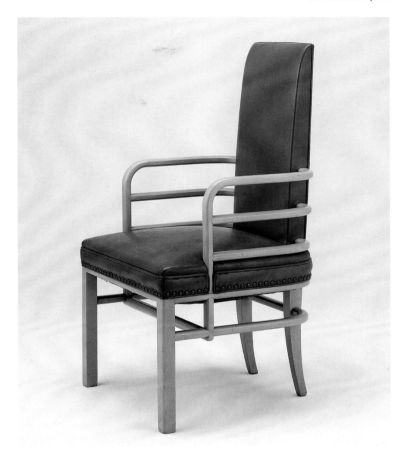

In the late 1920s and 1930s, the furniture and interiors of émigré designer Kem Weber were celebrated as original, colorful, and suited to the needs of modern living. Although he established his career in California rather than in New York City—then considered "the nation's style pulse"—critics compared his work favorably to that of his East Coast contemporaries.[1] In fact, Weber was praised as one of the first American designers to bring a "tradition-free, machine-age creativeness" to American interior design.[2] In 1931, a writer for *Creative Art* remarked: "As anyone knows who has followed the thirty years' war of Modernism versus the scattered remains of period heritage and comical restatements of these periods by the indefatigable machine, Kem Weber has been a consistent contributor to whatever excellent contemporary design has obtained in America."[3] Like Paul T. Frankl (see cat. no. 5), Weber sought to create forms that were devoid of historical references and suggestive of modern times. He embraced the machine not only for its ability to mass-produce objects and manipulate a variety of materials, but also because it symbolized both the rapid advance of technology and the shape of contemporary life itself.[4]

Although his early training in Germany taught him traditional cabinetmaking skills, Weber later excelled as the student and apprentice of Bruno Paul, the renowned designer and director of the Academy of Applied Arts in Berlin. It was at Paul's suggestion that Weber traveled to California to supervise construction of the German section of the 1915 "Panama-Pacific Exposition" in San Francisco; like Frankl, Weber was unable to return to Europe because of the political turmoil associated with the outbreak of World War I.[5] Weber decided to remain in California following this devastating turn of events, and began a career as an independent designer. Drawing upon

the instruction he received under Paul, he soon flourished as one of the few designers working in a modernist idiom in Los Angeles.

In 1921 Weber joined Barker Brothers, a prominent Los Angeles retail and interior design firm that designed and manufactured its own furniture and decorative accessories. Barker Brothers specialized in reproductions of English, French provincial, and Spanish furniture, but like many companies at this time, it retained a designer capable of offering modern alternatives to traditional styles (see also cat. nos. 3 and 9). Inspired by a visit to the "Exposition internationale des arts décoratifs et industriels modernes" in Paris, Weber returned to Los Angeles determined to promote the cause of modern design in the United States. Shortly thereafter, he established the Modes and Manners shop at Barker Brothers, which almost immediately became the principle source for Art Moderne and skyscraper-

inspired furniture and accessories on the West Coast.[6] Some of these products were custom-made according to Weber's designs,[7] and were thus undoubtedly more expensive than those—including the Art Institute's pieces—which he created for manufacturers such as the Grand Rapids Chair Company.

While Weber claimed that they "more truly express the American spirit than any other contemporary furniture that has been developed," his designs for Modes and Manners were influenced by his early training with Paul, as well as by the displays of French Art Moderne he would have seen at the Paris exposition; in fact, he asserted that he had sought to achieve in his work a balance between contemporary French and German designs, "keeping it simple and swift in line, not overly complicated, and yet giving it a certain rich elegance and comfort that is typically American."[8] Weber also worked as an interior designer for Barker Brothers, planning both totally modern homes and individual modern rooms in otherwise traditionally furnished residences, which were considered "the very smart thing among the fashionable people in California."[9] The success of his work may have prompted Weber to branch out on his own in 1927, when he resigned from Barker Brothers and opened an independent design studio in Hollywood.[10]

Although he achieved success in California, it was not until he became involved in several exhibits in New York that Weber became nationally accepted as a leader in the modern-design movement. For example, he was praised for his "Six in Three Rooms," exhibited at the R. H. Macy and Company department store in 1928. Here, Weber's designs were shown alongside the work of both Europeans such as Josef Hoffmann and Paul, and American designers such as Ilonka Karasz (see cat. no. 10) and Eugene Schoen (see cat. no. 6). In an attempt to design a space suited to the style and constraints of modern urban living, Weber exhibited an apartment comprising three multipurpose rooms: a combination dining alcove-kitchenette, bathroom-dressing room, and living room-bedroom.[11] Later, he participated in and helped organize New York exhibitions and publications sponsored by the influential American Union of Decorative Artists and Craftsmen (AUDAC). Similar to the American Designers' Gallery (see pp. 41–42), AUDAC brought together a number of architects, decorators, industrial designers, and other design professionals to organize exhibitions around their own work, with the goal of promulgating a style of American modernism.[12]

Weber also designed furniture for a number of manufacturers in Grand Rapids, Michigan, which disseminated his work to a wide audience. For example, in 1928 the Grand Rapids Chair Company introduced "The Kem

Weber Group"; it most likely included furniture such as the Art Institute's armchair and serving table, which were made as part of a nine-piece dining-room suite.[13] In this ensemble (fig. 1), Weber simplified traditional forms and, like other designers of the late 1920s, experimented with and combined both common and luxurious materials. The chair and table are characterized by horizontal planes that terminate in subtle curves and dramatic color contrasts. Weber emphasized the pieces' "sage-green" lacquer through a delicate use of silver leaf and "coral-red" leather upholstery, and his zig-zag decoration on the table's walnut frieze—undoubtedly executed by machine—adds spare ornament to an otherwise undecorated form.[14] While the striking colors and richly patterned walnut-veneer tabletop attest to Art Moderne's influence on Weber, the smoothly contoured members and corners of both pieces anticipate the sleek, tubular-metal furniture that characterized the American streamlined aesthetic of the 1930s.[15]

Figure 1

Kem Weber (American, born Germany; 1889–1963) Dining-room suite from "The Kem Weber Group," c. 1928. Made by Grand Rapids Chair Company, Grand Rapids, Mich. Photo: *Creative Art* 7, 4 (Oct. 1930), p. 253.

Modern Solutions

Whereas the "modernistic" merely touches the external aspects in surface pattern, the modern solution is based upon the three vital elements of design—materials, tools, and purposes.

Donald Deskey[1]

In the 1930s, many Americans continued to prefer the safety and exclusivity associated with handmade, tradition-based objects such as Danish silver (see cat. no. 15), Swedish glass (see cat. no. 17), and even French Art Moderne objects. Many others, however, desired functional, informal modernist furnishings that were mass-manufactured from affordable materials. Machine-made decorative wares were by no means a new phenomenon in the 1930s; during the previous decade, designers such as Gene Theobald (see cat. no. 9) and Kem Weber (see cat. no. 11) had encouraged machine production by creating works for large manufacturing companies. Following the economic collapse of 1929, however, a number of factors, including the growth of the industrial-design profession, new developments in transportation, and events such as Chicago's "Century of Progress International Exposition" (1933–34), suggested the machine's immense economic, scientific, and social potential, and inspired a new streamlined look that was soon applied to all realms of design.

Many modern designers in the 1930s created objects that readily lent themselves to machine manufacture and echoed the sleek, mechanized look of the machine itself. Following the lead of progressive European counterparts such as the Swiss architect Le Corbusier, whose seminal *Towards a New Architecture* was published in English in 1927, American practitioners hoped to establish a style that, in the words of author Jeffrey L. Meikle, progressed "from the random uncertainties of life to the reliability of the perfect machine."[2] Streamlined objects were characterized by an extreme paring down of forms, by continuous, uninterrupted lines, and by their use of industrial materials such as chrome-plated metal, stainless steel, and molded wood. In conceiving them, their designers rejected the profuse patterning, austere geometries, and rich materials of Art Deco, and chose instead to imitate the smooth, aerodynamic forms of the new airplanes, automobiles, and trains that were at once revolutionizing travel and bolstering America's sense of national accomplishment.

This new design idiom was popularized by industrial designers, who gave many commercial and domestic products a fresh, machinelike appearance in order to enhance their appeal to consumers.[3] Charged with interior and graphic design as well, these professionals—most often architects who turned to design due to the decline in new construction during the Depression—responded to the rapid spread of electricity and the corresponding growth of the household appliance industry by introducing a multitude of streamlined objects, from pencil sharpeners to kitchen equipment, into American homes and offices.[4]

A major public venue for machine-inspired design was the "Century of Progress International Exposition." The Chicago fair, which bore the motto "See America Streamlined," celebrated the city's centennial by glorifying scientific progress through sleek displays and products that exhibitors hoped would instill a sense of optimism in Depression-weary Americans (see Barter, p. 14). Just as impressive were the model homes built of different materials, such as the glass-and-steel "Crystal House," the "Lumber Industries House," the "Masonite House," and George Fred and William Keck's famous copper, glass, and steel "House of Tomorrow."[5] A number of these residences, including the "House of Tomorrow," were outfitted with a pastiche of traditional and Art Moderne–inspired furnishings.

The majority of the exposition's model homes and other buildings, however—including the "House of Tomorrow" (fig. 1)—incorporated tubular, chrome-plated-steel and bent-aluminum furniture made by firms such as the Howell Company (see cat. no. 13). Despite earlier efforts by designers such as Donald Deskey to incorporate chrome-plated and aluminum furniture into interiors (see cat. no. 7), few

Americans had seen effective displays of metal furniture before the Chicago fair. In fact, as recently as 1929, such pieces had generally been considered appropriate only as "office equipment, " their use in domestic settings derided as "robot modernism."[6] The "Century of Progress Exposition," however, made a profound impact upon the psyche of both manufacturers and consumers: its abundant displays of metal furniture for both indoor and outdoor use helped create an increased supply of such pieces, and encouraged home and business owners to purchase them.

Despite the popularity of streamlining, however, critics began to complain that it had become a mere marketing tool that was superficially applied—like the cubistic decoration of the 1920s—to a myriad of objects.[7] The emerging notion among American designers that function was "the underlying principle of all beautiful utilitarian objects"[8] coincided with the growing influence of German Bauhaus architects, artists, and designers such as László Moholy-Nagy and Ludwig Mies van der Rohe, who fled to the United States after Hitler came to power in 1933. These designers believed that the machine should be used to render standardized forms that were "determined by use . . . influenced by material . . . the result of some process of manufacture . . . [and] the creation of the designer."[9] Although such functionalist approaches informed the cantilevered, tubular-metal furniture that Mies produced in the 1920s (see fig. 2), they were not actively promoted in the United States until the 1930s, when International Style architecture and Bauhaus ideologies were disseminated by recently established schools such as the New Bauhaus in Chicago (1937), and exhibitions such as "Modern Architecture: International Exhibition" (1932), "Machine Art," (1934), and "Bauhaus 1919–1928" (1938) at the Museum of Modern Art, New York.

Figure 1

George Fred Keck (American; 1895–1980) and William Keck (American; born 1908). Dining room, "House of Tomorrow," at the "Century of Progress International Exposition," Chicago, Ill., 1933. Chicago Historical Society, Hedrich-Blessing Archive.

The widespread promotion of these ideals, together with the public interest generated in metal furniture by the 1933 exposition, and the increased technological capabilities of the machine itself, made it possible for designers to accomplish what had eluded Deskey in the late 1920s. By the mid-1930s, metal furniture had become almost as familiar as wood in "every kind of interior from penthouse to chain cafeteria, from intercity bus to country church."[10] Many pieces, such as Wolfgang Hoffmann's cocktail table (cat. no. 13), for example, were well-designed and mass produced; they were, moreover, sold at reasonable prices, which became increasingly important during and after the Depression years. Metal furniture, the pinnacle of high-modern design, was also custom-created by designers such as Warren McArthur (see cat. no. 12), and conceived for integrated interiors by architects such as Frank Lloyd Wright and Richard Neutra (see cat. no. 14).

In sharp contrast to the clean anonymity of streamlined styles and Bauhaus functionalism, Scandinavian organicism emerged as a design alternative in the 1930s, and remained popular through the 1940s, influencing the work of American designers such as Russel Wright (see cat. no. 16), Charles and Ray Eames (see cat. no. 22), and Oscar Riedener (see cat. no. 25). Often executed in warm-toned woods, organic designs were characterized by undulating lines, curving silhouettes, and rounded corners based on natural forms. Organicism, which like other forms of modernism was concerned with the "harmonious integration of the parts within the whole,"[11] was popularized by the buildings and furniture of the Finnish architect Alvar Aalto (see cat. no. 19, fig. 1), whose famous "Finnish Pavilion" at the 1939 New York World's Fair was instrumental in introducing the style to American audiences.[12] America's growing fascination with organic

design was further encouraged by the 1940 exhibit "Organic Design in Home Furnishings," held at the Museum of Modern Art (see cat. no. 22). Although created by machine, organic designs were regarded by many critics and consumers as a more human approach to modernism, a relief from the sometimes cold and clinical feel of machine-inspired designs.

Figure 2

Ludwig Mies van der Rohe (American, born Germany; 1886–1969). *Armchair*, 1927. Chrome-plated steel and leather; 80 x 54 x 85.1 cm (31½ x 21¼ x 33½ in.). The Art Institute of Chicago, restricted gift of Graham Foundation for Advanced Studies in the Fine Arts (1970.403).

12. **Warren McArthur**

(American; 1885–1961)

Side Chair, c. 1936

Made by Warren McArthur Corporation, Rome,
New York

Anodized aluminum with original cotton
upholstery; 80 x 43.2 x 48.3 cm (32½ x 17 x 19 in.)

On underside of seat: Warren McArthur
Corporation label

Restricted gift of Mrs. Robert O. Delaney, 2000.341

During the 1930s, Chicago-born engineer and designer Warren McArthur created metal furniture for both residential and commercial use. Distinguished from the tubular-steel furniture of the Bauhaus designers by its matte, anodized-aluminum material and innovative construction techniques, McArthur's spare designs not only exemplify the contemporary machine aesthetic, but embody the craft tradition as well.[1] This elegant side chair epitomizes the designer's oeuvre. Although its smooth, streamlined look suggests machine manufacture, it was in fact custom-made: assembled by hand, the hollow-aluminum members are not welded together, but rather connected by internal tension rods and secured by ring joints. McArthur promoted and relied on interchangeable parts, drawing upon a select repertoire of aluminum sections in order to facilitate "the creation of an infinite variety of styles, applicable to any need, in business or in the home."[2] Although McArthur's inventive furniture was quite individual when it was made, it also followed contemporary modern-design trends. While his pieces are extremely sympathetic to the streamlined metal furniture popularized in the United States during the 1930s, the fact that they were not mass-produced—but instead made-to-order for an elite clientele—aligns them with the sumptuous, often exclusive objects produced during the 1920s (see, for example, cat. no. 6).

In 1930, the designer founded the Warren McArthur Corporation, his own furniture-making concern, in Los Angeles, later moving the business to Rome, New York, and opening a showroom on Manhattan's Park Avenue.[3] In New York, McArthur perfected the ring-joint construction technique seen in the Art Institute's chair, and also received prestigious, nationwide contracts from a number of private individuals and large companies. He designed furniture, for example, for the dining cars of the Union Pacific Railroad, the corporate headquarters of the Chrysler Corporation in Detroit, and the lavish beauty salon at Chicago's Marshall Field and Company department store.[4] Around 1936, moreover, he developed prototype models of an armchair, desk, and table for Frank Lloyd Wright's Johnson Wax Administration Building in Racine, Wisconsin (see cat. no. 14, fig. 2). Although the contract for the building's furniture was ultimately awarded to the Metal Office Furniture Company of Grand Rapids, Michigan, McArthur's armchair represents a fascinating counterpoint to the manufactured pieces, one of which is in the Art Institute's collection (see cat. no. 14).

McArthur seems to have employed only metal in his furniture designs. His earliest plans were executed in copper and in stainless steel, which was frequently used in the streamlined furniture that achieved popularity in 1930s America. Anodized aluminum, however, soon proved to be McArthur's material of choice, not only because of its durable, lightweight, and malleable qualities, but also because its brushed surfaces provided an appealing alternative to the sterile coldness of steel and chromium.[5] The designer advertised his aluminum as "next in hardness to the diamond, [possessing a] velvety soft, smooth feel of satin silver," and praised his anodizing process, which involved electrolytically coating a metal surface with a protective oxide, as capable of rendering his furniture "untarnishable."[6]

The modern simplicity and usefulness of McArthur's furniture made it appropriate for many settings. The Art Institute's chair, for example, promoted as a "featherweight beauty—six pounds of slender, captivating charm," was undoubtedly suitable for dining, and was used in Chicago establishments such as Harry's New York Bar.[7] A contemporary photograph of the bar's interior (fig. 1) shows

several chairs identical to this one, as well as sofas, tables, and ashtray stands, all designed by McArthur and fabricated from his standardized aluminum components. In this piece, McArthur echoes the subtle curve of the backrest in both the crest rail and the stretcher between the front legs, and harmonizes the aluminum's soft tone with the olive-green color of the original upholstered seat.[8] Available in a wide variety of colors, the chair was listed in the Warren McArthur Corporation 1938 price list for twenty-eight dollars— which would have made it less affordable to consumers than other contemporary objects such as Wolfgang Hoffmann's chrome-plated-steel and glass table (see cat. no. 13).[9]

Figure 1

Harry's New York Bar, Chicago, Ill., c. 1936. Chicago Historical Society, Hedrich-Blessing Archive.

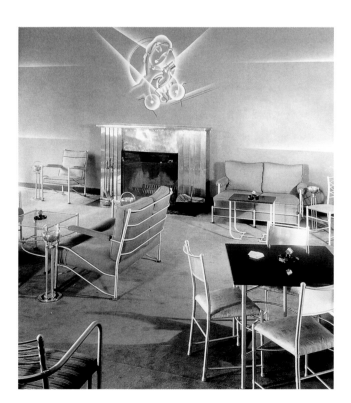

13. **Wolfgang Hoffmann**

(American, born Austria; 1900–1969)

Table, 1934/35

Made by Howell Company, St. Charles, Illinois
Chrome-plated steel and glass; h. 43.2 cm
(17 in.) x diam. 62 cm (24⁵/₈ in.)
Restricted gift of Fern and Manfred Steinfeld,
1988.450

The son of Josef Hoffmann, renowned Viennese architect, designer, and founding member of the Wiener Werkstätte, Wolfgang Hoffmann immigrated to New York City in 1925, and established his own reputation as a designer of Werkstätte-inspired interiors and accessories. The pewter cigarette-holder-and-ashtray ensembles he designed with his wife and early creative partner, Pola, for example, were undoubtedly influenced both by the Hoffmanns' early training and by the contemporary American fascination with Viennese design, and recall the geometric shapes favored by the Wiener Werkstätte.[1]

Hoffmann is remembered less for these early creations, however, than he is for his later, solo work as a designer of mass-produced metal furniture. In 1929, a critic for *Good Furniture Magazine* wrote that "some of the best designers of modern art for American use, insist that we are going to see a greater use of metal than ever before."[2] Such indeed became the case during the Great Depression and throughout the 1930s, when mass-produced metal furniture was thought to glorify rapid, machine manufacture; provide a more affordable alternative to wood (it required less, if any, handwork); and herald a new manifestation of modernity rooted in the technological advance of industry and transportation. At the 1933 "Century of Progress International Exposition" in Chicago, for example, audiences encountered these ideas by visiting various exhibition buildings decorated almost entirely with metal furniture.[3]

The prolific use of metal furnishings in the fair's fourteen model houses was unprecedented, and helped to establish metal furniture as a vital component in the modern American home (see p. 48, fig. 1). The Howell Company of Geneva, Illinois, which proclaimed itself the "originator of the modern metal furniture idea in America," provided a number of these model residences with its tubular, "Chromsteel" (chromium-plated steel) furniture.[4] By 1928, the company had begun to manufacture its own version of the cantilevered, tubular-steel chairs first produced by Bauhaus designers Marcel Breuer and Ludwig Mies van der Rohe (see Barter, fig. 3, and p. 49, fig. 2), and soon added tubular-steel armchairs and settees that were chrome-plated for indoor use, and enameled for outdoor use.[5] When Howell's president,

William McCredie, saw Hoffmann's interior designs for the "Lumber Industries House" at the 1933 exposition, where Hoffmann also assisted Joseph Urban in developing the fair's dramatic color schemes,[6] he hired Hoffmann to design exclusively for his company, which sought a modern designer to strengthen its growing line. Hoffmann subsequently moved to Illinois, where he supervised the manufacture of his designs until 1942.[7]

Like Warren McArthur's furniture (see cat. no. 12), Hoffmann's work for Howell included a variety of metal chairs and tables intended for both residential and commercial use. While all of his creations were distinguished by their flat- or tubular-metal members, Hoffmann often incorporated colorful, imitation-leather Fabrikoid® upholstery into his chairs and sofas, and designed tables with a range of glass tops, and black tops made from Formica® or linoleum.[8] The Art Institute's round table, for instance, combines four steel bars that are connected by double cross-braces and surmounted by a glass top; Hoffmann did not attempt to disguise the table's construction, and actually drew attention to it through details such as visible screws. While Howell also sold a rectangular version of this design (see fig. 1), which most likely functioned as a coffee or side table, the Art Institute's piece was probably used as a cocktail table. The Prohibition era (1920–33) saw the rise of a number of new social customs such as the private cocktail party, which created the need for novel furniture forms. Cocktail tables typically featured glass tops that resisted ring-stains from glasses, and were kept low to the ground so that a hostess could serve guests in comfort. As Paul T. Frankl suggested in 1928, "low tables connote informality, recumbent or semi-recumbent intimacy—in a word, complete relaxation."[9]

Unlike custom-made metal furniture created by designers such as McArthur and

Richard Neutra (see cat. no. 14), Hoffmann's table represents an example of simplified, mass-produced metal furnishings that were readily available to many Americans. Whereas McArthur's side chair (cat. no. 12) sold for twenty-eight dollars at about the same time, comparable pieces in the Howell catalogue sold for thirteen to fifteen dollars.[10] The Howell Company also marketed its furniture to a wider audience than did McArthur; the firm had showrooms in New York, Chicago, San Francisco, and Los Angeles, and also distributed their merchandise through "dealers [and] decorators."[11] In 1936, writers Sheldon Cheney and Martha Candler Cheney celebrated partnerships such as Hoffmann's and Howell's. Working together, the Cheneys suggested, designers and large-scale manufacturers could produce furnishings "on a scale which will soon permit the homemaker in the most remote part of the country to plan her own interiors representative of modern design." "Provided only that she has a reasonable budget and fundamentally sound personal taste," they continued, "she can obtain well-designed pieces or sets representing any reasonable degree of simplicity or luxury."[12]

Figure 1

Howell Company, *Modern Chromsteel Furniture Catalog #18.* (St. Charles, Ill., 1937), p. 31.

14. **Frank Lloyd Wright**

(American; 1867–1959)

Armchair and Desk, 1936/39

Made by Metal Office Furniture Company
(later Steelcase, Incorporated),
Grand Rapids, Michigan
Armchair: painted steel tubing, maple armrests,
original upholstery; 85.7 x 60.3 x 54.6 cm
(34³/₄ x 23³/₄ x 21¹/₂ in.)
Desk: painted steel tubing, maple work surface,
with later laminated surface; 96.5 x 212.7 x 138.8 cm
(38 x 83³/₄ x 54⁵/₈ in.)
Gift of the Johnson Wax Company, 1972.310–11

Richard J. Neutra

(American, born Austria; 1892–1970)

Armchair, c. 1930

Los Angeles, California
Chrome-plated steel, replacement upholstery;
86.4 x 57.2 x 73.6 cm (34 x 22¹/₂ x 29 in.)
Gift of Herschel A. Elarth in honor of Dione and
Richard J. Neutra, F.A.I.A., 1987.182

Architects Frank Lloyd Wright and Richard J. Neutra created some of the most important American buildings of the first half of the twentieth century; their furniture designs, including the tubular-steel pieces shown here, were not mass-produced, but rather planned and executed for these specific environments.[1] Wright conceived his patented ergonomic desk and chair for his Johnson Wax Administration Building (Racine, Wisconsin; 1936–39), while Neutra intended his armchair, with its patented steel-spring support, to be used in several of his interiors, including his own Los Angeles home and studio (1932), and the ticket office for the Catalina Island ferry, which he designed in 1937.[2] Although highly original, these examples of Wright's and Neutra's work reflect prominent design ideals of the day: streamlined in form, they were made to correspond with their architectural surroundings.

Celebrated for creative designs that made innovative use of materials and space, both men embraced the notion of a totally integrated environment. In 1908, for instance, Wright wrote of his desire to make "a building, together with its equipment, appurtenances, and environment, an entity which shall constitute a complete work of art."[3] He introduced this concept to Americans through his Prairie School homes in Chicago and Oak Park, Illinois, into which he incorporated furnishings, metalwork, and stained glass of his own design. Although Wright's early furniture embodies the reformist impulses of both the English and American Arts and Crafts movements, which promoted "honestly constructed" forms unfettered by unnecessary ornament, Wright never condemned the machine as a means of production. Instead, he believed that "the art of the future will be the expression of the individual artist through the thousand powers of the machine, the machine, doing all those things that the individual workman cannot do."[4]

Furthermore, he maintained that the beauty of an object was a result of the design, and that the machine could be used to bring forth the inherent possibilities of many materials.[5]

In order to produce a completely synthesized atmosphere in the Johnson Wax headquarters, Wright designed the building's interior elements, including the heating systems, "mushroom" columns, skylights, light fixtures, and furniture, which included three- and four-legged chairs, and nine variations of a desk intended to accommodate different office tasks.[6] Although Wright initially planned to produce his designs in sheet aluminum, its prohibitive costs rendered it an impractical choice; in the end, tubular steel was selected as an alternative, and prototypes were submitted by both Warren McArthur (fig. 2) and the Metal Office Furniture Company, to which Wright ultimately awarded the contract.[7] While Wright may have decided upon tubular steel due to its fashionable connotations, he most likely chose it because it was extremely durable and more economical than aluminum.

Wright designed a main work space for the Johnson Wax headquarters, as he had done

Figure 1

Interior of Main Workroom Looking Towards Lobby, S.C. Johnson and Son, Incorporated, Racine, Wisc., 1936–39. Ryerson Library Photo Collection, The Art Institute of Chicago.

with his earlier Larkin Building in Buffalo, New York (1903–04), and it is for this Great Room (fig. 1) that the Art Institute's pieces were made.[8] The furniture was remarkably sympathetic to the building itself: its red color, carried over onto the matching upholstery, echoes the brick used on the structure's exterior, and its rounded, cantilevered shapes mimic the Great Room's mushroom columns. The desk and armchair are also extremely functional and ergonomic: the desk's vast, smooth, multi-level top provided ample working space, and its tubular frame supports a hanging wastebasket and drawer unit. Wright designed the three-legged chair to allow employees free movement of their feet, and to encourage good posture; if not sat in correctly, it would tip over.[9]

Neutra's furniture, like Wright's, was most often custom-made for the buildings he designed.[10] Trained in the Viennese architectural tradition, he was nonetheless undoubtedly influenced by Wright, for whom he worked from 1924 to 1925. In the Art Institute's innovative chair, Neutra imitates the design of his own buildings, which were associated with the International Style of architecture, and celebrated in the Museum of Modern Art, New York's "Modern Architecture: International Exhibition" of 1932 (see p. 48.) At this groundbreaking show, several of Neutra's building designs were displayed alongside those of Le Corbusier, Gropius, Mies van der Rohe, and Wright, including that of the Lovell House, Los Angeles (1929), which was praised as "the most advanced house built in America since the War."[11]

Neutra himself was labeled "the leading architect of the West Coast," and "second only to Wright in his international reputation."[12] Critics compared his work favorably to that of the Bauhaus architects, and his design for the Art Institute's chair is indebted to Bauhaus faculty such as Mies and Breuer, who designed cantilevered, tubular-steel chairs in 1927 and 1928, respectively.[13] Nevertheless, the steel-spring support on Neutra's chair is highly inventive, and testifies to his originality as a designer. Two loose cushions are fitted between the continuous pieces of streamlined metal that form the chair's arms and legs, and are adjustable within the frame. They rest upon a curved, resilient, steel-spring support bar, which is attached to the front rail beneath the seat. Originally designed with a metal frame, this chair pattern was later made with a wooden frame balanced on the steel support.[14] Above all, Neutra engineered this chair for comfort; its deep seat and wide cushions allowed the sitter to relax in an unrestrained, informal, and distinctly modern style. Like Wolfgang Hoffmann's small table (cat. no. 12), Neutra's low-slung chair was inspired by the aesthetic of comfort that began in the late 1920s, and flourished after World War II in the work of designers such as Charles and Ray Eames (see cat. no. 22).

Figure 2
Warren McArthur (American; 1885–1961). Prototype Chair for S. C. Johnson and Son, Incorporated, Racine, Wisc., c. 1936. Media; 81.3 x 59.1 x 45.7 (32 x 23¼ x 18 in). Wolfsonian-Florida International University, Miami Beach, Mitchell Wolfson, Jr. Collection.

15. **Peer Smed**

(American, born Denmark; 1878–1943)

Candelabra, 1934

Brooklyn, New York

Silver; 47.3 x 28.6 cm (18 5/8 x 11 1/4 in.)

Stamped on underside of base: *STERLING/PEER SMED/1934*

Wesley M. Dixon, Jr. and Mr. and Mrs. Albert Pick, Jr. funds, 1989.516.1–2

Compote, 1933

Brooklyn, New York

Silver; h. 17.8 (7 in.) x diam. (top) 15.8 cm (6 3/8 in.)

Stamped on underside of base: *STERLING/PEER SMED/1933*

Gift of the Antiquarian Society through the Mr. and Mrs. James W. Alsdorf Fund, 1986.1061

During the 1930s, when modern, afford-able, and easily maintained materials such as silver-plated metals and aluminum were mass-produced and marketed throughout the United States, metalsmith Peer Smed disa-vowed machine manufacture and relied upon the techniques of handcraftsmanship that he learned in his native Denmark. Remembered in 1947 as "a tall, robust Viking-type of man with an enormous head of hair and a long red-dish beard,"[1] Smed employed Scandinavian metalsmiths in his Brooklyn atelier, and per-mitted no division of labor: each piece was to be made by one smith alone.[2] In his "barnlike workshop at the end of an alley," as one observer described it, Smed created decorative ironwork, and silver flatware, holloware, and jewelry, all clearly inspired by the designs of Danish sil-versmiths such as Georg Jensen.[3]

Although he reportedly made "royal household pieces" for the "Kings of Denmark and Sweden," little is known about Smed's life and career until the 1930s.[4] Before immigrating to the United States around 1904, however, he

Figure 1

Georg Jensen (Danish; 1866–1935). *Compote with Grapes, No. 263,* 1918. Silver. Stockholm, the National Swedish Art Museums.

studied with the renowned metalworker A. Michelsen in Copenhagen, and was undoubtedly inspired by the highly stylized floral and vegetal motifs employed by his Danish contemporaries.[5] After settling in New York, Smed did not attempt to create an American style of silver as did fellow émigré Erik Magnussen (see cat. no. 3), but instead continued to use the foliate motifs—and more abstract shapes and scrolls—seen in the Danish silver wares that were exhibited and enthusiastically embraced in America during the 1920s and 1930s.[6]

Smed, like his Scandinavian counterparts, manipulated silver to its best advantage, creating resplendent forms such as the Art Institute's compote and candelabra. Although derived from traditional shapes and inspired by Danish models, each work bears Smed's own stylistic imprint; his soft, flowing lines and natural motifs are less stylized and ornate than some Danish designs (see fig. 1), for example, and convey an overall sense of modernist

restraint. In the compote, a plantlike stem rises from the hand-hammered surface of the base, and appears to blossom into the open-bud shape that forms the bowl. Delicate beading on the stem, floral ornament on the bowl, and an undulating rim add to the piece's organic character. Similarly, the stalklike arms of the triple-branch candelabra sprout from a spherical center section, which Smed joined to the hand-hammered base with a ring of scrolling leaves.

It might be expected that the Arts and Crafts practice of hand metalworking would have fallen out of favor by the 1930s, a victim of machine production, mass consumption, and the Depression.[7] While the streamlined aesthetic pervaded advertising, domestic, and transportation design, the public, however, continued to associate expensive, handmade silver with tradition and affluence, and it remained desirable to those who could afford it. Indeed, with critics charging that the rise of machine manufacture had contributed to a "lack of really new and native impulses of design," handmade Danish and Swedish work came to be lauded as "the only modern silver that [seems] to succeed in being modern and at the same time to retain something of the flowing graciousness that the metal silver naturally has as its birthright."[8]

16. Russel Wright

(American; 1904–1976)

"Oceana" Box, 1935

Made by Klise Manufacturing Company,
Grand Rapids, Michigan
Blond maple, hinged lid; 7.6 x 23.5 x 15.9 cm
(3 x 9¼ x 6¼ in.)
Incised on base: facsimile signature,
Russel Wright; printed on adhesive label on base:
designed by Russel Wright/"Oceana"
carved wooden ware made by KLISE
Martha and William Steen funds, 1999.679

"American Modern" Dinnerware, 1937

Made by Steubenville Pottery, Steubenville, Ohio
Glazed earthenware; Pitcher: 27 x 21.6 x 16.8 cm
(10⅝ x 8½ x 6⅝ in.), 1995.246; Celery dish:
3.2 x 33.7 x 9.2 cm (1¼ x 13¼ x 3⅝ in.), 1995.250;
Sauce boat: 6.4 x 22.9 x 16.5 cm (2½ x 9 x 6½ in.),
1995.251a; Sauce underplate: 2.5 x 27.6 x 15.9 cm
(1 x 10⅞ x 6¼ in.), 1996.251b; Salt and pepper
shakers (each): h. 5.4 x (2⅛ in.) x diam. 5.4 cm
(2⅛ in.), 1996.449–.450; Covered casserole dish:
10.2 x 29.9 x 20.3 cm (4 x 11 x 8 in.), 1999.249a–b
Gift of Beryl C. Michels

Both Russel Wright's "American Modern" dinnerware pattern and his "Oceana" box (part of a larger group of home furnishings called "American Way") display his mastery of the organic, Scandinavian-inspired designs popularized in the mid-1930s through the 1940s. Both of these lines, characterized by undulating and often idiosyncratic shapes, were intended for informal household use. Through such objects, Wright promoted his vision of a more relaxed domestic environment, which included informal, inexpensive furnishings.[1] Indeed, Wright's design philosophy was egalitarian, and he meant for his works, including the Art Institute's "Oceana" box and "American Modern" wares, to be enjoyed and appreciated by a broad audience of middle-class American consumers.[2] In order to achieve this objective and produce objects that might "facilitate the way of ease . . . of living by design," he introduced lines of dinnerware, glassware, flatware, furniture, and accessories that were efficient, aesthetically and ergonomically pleasing, and reasonably priced.[3]

Wright's early interest in theatrical design shaped his career as an industrial designer and introduced him to prominent personalities in the field; in 1924, for example, he began an apprenticeship under the American stage and industrial designer Norman Bel Geddes.[4] Three years later, Wright married sculpture student Mary Small Einstein, who encouraged him to adapt his knowledge of stage design to the production of decorative objects for retail sale. The couple soon entered into a fruitful business partnership in which Russel designed while Mary concentrated on marketing his work. Wright's experiments with various forms and materials, beginning with spun-aluminum and pewter dining accessories in the early 1930s, were extremely well received, and enhanced his reputation as an original and inventive designer. Not only did he participate in several prominent exhibitions, including the annual "Exhibition of Contemporary Industrial Design" at the Metropolitan Museum of Art, New York, in 1931, and the Philadelphia Museum of Art's 1932 "Machine Art" show, but also found work designing furniture and metalwork for manufacture.[5]

Wright designed the "Oceana" line for the Klise Manufacturing Company of Grand Rapids, Michigan, in 1935. These free-form serving pieces, which include star- and shell-shaped dishes, were inspired by marine motifs and executed in various woods, including cherry, gum, hazelwood, and blond maple. The Art Institute's box possesses a richly organic quality thanks to its warm, natural-wood texture, smooth, rounded edges, and a hinged top that suggests an ocean wave. Although produced by a woodworking machine, this piece, most likely intended to hold candy, has a handmade, sculptural presence.[6]

Included in Wright's larger "American Way" group of home furnishings, the "Oceana" line was publicized as an affordable, modern American design that existed without reference to European precedent.[7] "Oceana" was officially validated as a premier example of functional, modern design when two of its offerings—a box identical to the Art Institute's, and a centerpiece bowl—were featured on the cover of the January 1940 issue of *The Bulletin of The Museum of Modern Art* as representative examples from the museum's "Useful Objects Under Ten Dollars" exhibition. This display included "a small group of many well-designed objects," each chosen on the basis of its "suitability to purpose; suitability to material; suitability to process of manufacture; and aesthetic quality."[8] Since buyers apparently felt that it was only appropriate for use in beach and resort homes, however, "Oceana" failed to meet sales expectations, and was discontinued in 1940.

In sharp contrast, Wright's "American Modern" line of colorful, whimsical earthenware proved to be the most popular ceramic dinnerware ever created. The designer's sculptural training is evident in the soft, undulating, rimless shapes of "American Modern"; just as other designers applied Cubist features to decorative forms in the 1920s (see cat. nos. 7, 8), Wright's fluid forms suggest his knowledge of Surrealist painting. The late 1930s saw an explosion of color on the American tableware market as a result of intense competition between numerous manufacturers; in around 1935, for example, Frederick Hurten Rhead designed his "Fiesta Ware" table service in vivid shades of blue, green, ivory, orange-red, and yellow.[9] Wright's more subdued colors, such as "Granite Grey" and "Seafoam Blue," were the result of glaze experiments; although he followed the contemporary color trend, Wright's softened hues were primarily inspired by nature.[10] He intended these shades to be used interchangeably, in a mix-and-match fashion. Many newlyweds selected "American Modern" in the final years of the Depression, when the availability of inexpensive, sixteen-piece starter sets prompted buyers to complete their services from open stock.

Beginning in 1939, Steubenville Pottery successfully marketed and manufactured the service for over two decades. "American Modern" remained popular through the 1950s, and Wright elaborated the line by adding table linens (1946–48), glassware, and stainless-steel flatware (1951) to its offerings.[11] That the pattern's biomorphic forms remained fashionable for so long was undoubtedly due to the proliferation of organically inspired decorative arts, such as Eva Zeisel's *"Museum" Coffeepot* (cat. no. 23), in the years after World War II. Although Wright followed "American Modern" with several dinnerware services, including "Casual China" (1946) and the plastic lines "Residential" (1953) and "Flair" (1959), none of these achieved the widespread acclaim of "American Modern."[12]

17. Sidney B. Waugh

(American; 1904–1963)

Trident Punch Bowl, 1935

Made by Steuben Glass, Division of Corning Glass
Works, Corning, New York
Glass, blown and engraved; h. 26 cm (10¼ in.) x
diam. (top) 36.1 cm (14³⁄₁₆ in.)
Gift of Robert Allerton, 1938.214

Zodiac Bowl, 1935

Made by Steuben Glass, Division of Corning Glass
Works, Corning, New York
Engraved by J. Libisch (American; act. 1930s)
Glass, blown and engraved; diam. 40.6 cm (16 in.)
Signed on underside of rim: *Sidney Waugh
Steuben; 1937; J. Libisch*
Gift of Mr. and Mrs. Hugh J. Smith, Jr., 1950.1160

Paul Manship

(American; 1885–1966)

Vase, 1937/40

Made by Steuben Glass, Division of Corning Glass
Works, Corning, New York
Glass; blown and engraved; h. 35.5 cm (14 in.) x
diam. 20.7 cm (8⅛ in.)
Signed on body: *Paul Manship*; signed around
pontil: *Steuben 1940 #4 of 6 Manship*
Gift of Mrs. William H. Stanley, 1961.428

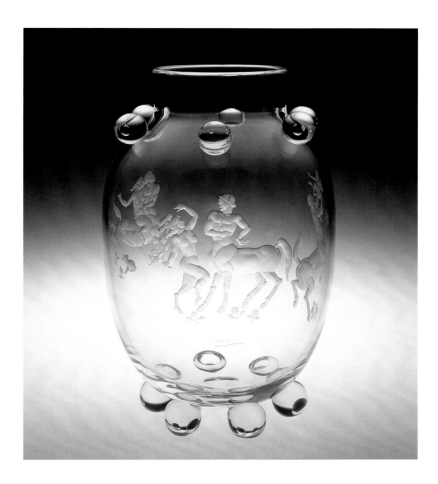

Steuben Glass, a subsidiary of Corning Glass Works, was founded in 1903 by the English-born glassmaker Frederick Carder. Initially devoted to the manufacture of colorful and sinuous Art Nouveau–inspired glassware, Carder's enterprise faltered around the time of the 1929 stock-market crash. Steuben suffered not only from ineffective management, poor quality control, and a lack of artistic focus—the company made everything from architectural glass panels to tableware—but also from Carder's promotion of an outmoded style. The firm was reorganized in 1933 under Arthur A. Houghton, Jr., a young Corning director who envisioned a new Steuben capable of creating the finest glass in the world. With this goal in mind, he hired architect John Monteith Gates as Steuben's new managing director; Gates in turn recruited sculptor Sidney B. Waugh to join Steuben as chief designer.[1] Gates was undoubtedly drawn to Waugh because of his skill with three-dimensional materials, a knowledge he brought to bear on the form and decoration of glass as well as bronze and stone.

With Gates and Waugh on board, Houghton revealed a new leaded-glass formula that Corning chemists had developed around 1930; iron impurities were removed from this colorless material, which has an extremely high refractive quality that allows the whole spectrum of light, including the ultraviolet, to pass through. Steuben touted this new substance, often called "crystal"

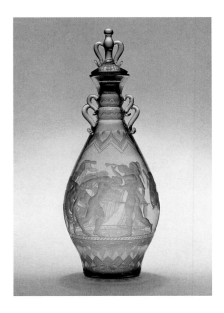

because of its brilliant resemblance to rock crystal, as "probably the clearest and most transparent material produced by man and more free from flaws and imperfections than any glass now made or produced heretofore."[2] Waugh created new, modern design schemes to take full advantage of the glass's clarity, and the company's subsequent success prompted Houghton to discontinue Steuben's original, colorful wares.

Steuben opened a New York showroom and outlet in 1934, and established a genuine design department a year later, when Gates hired six recent graduates from architectural schools as designers. Following Waugh's lead, these designers created simple, neoclassical and mythological decorative scenes that were skillfully engraved onto the thick, heavy glass. Steuben's artists were intensely reliant on the luxurious Swedish glass exhibited at world's fairs and American museums in the 1920s; Swedish glass was shown, for example, at the 1925 Paris exposition. Sweden's hand-blown glass vessels of the 1920s not only reflect the influence of that country's eighteenth-century neoclassical architecture, but also allude to the international use of neoclassical decorative motifs during that time, which were applied to everything from Swedish glass and French furniture to American silver (see cat. no. 3). Furthermore, the exquisitely engraved glass of Sweden's Orrefors factory—as well as ceramics, furniture, metalwork, and textiles—was shown in "Swedish Contemporary Decorative Arts," an exhibition that appeared at both The Art Institute of Chicago and The Metropolitan Museum of Art, New York, in 1927 (see Barter, fig. 8).[4] This endorsement by museums such as the Art Institute may have underscored the elitist associations Swedish glass elicited in the United States, and certainly contributed to a retail success that Steuben hoped to duplicate with its own wares in the 1930s.[5] Although

Steuben's wares may have been considered slightly outmoded due to their heavy, Art Moderne–influenced ornament, they were extremely popular among tradition-oriented, affluent clientele. Steuben hired a team of Swedish glassblowers to supervise hand production, and was able to market its products as luxury items even in the midst of the Great Depression.

In 1935, the company exhibited fifteen pieces of its new, colorless glass in New York and London, where critics greeted it with acclaim, and heralded it as "[purely] American in character," "the clearest crystal glass the world has ever known."[6] Waugh's *Trident Punch Bowl* and *Zodiac Bowl* designs were both displayed, and were lauded for the balance they achieved between classically inspired engraved decoration and smooth, modern expanses of undecorated, colorless glass. Waugh formed his punch bowl's well-proportioned body by inventively balancing a large, volumetric shape on a smaller, inverted bowl. His engraved decoration, described as floating "like a frosty pattern on a windowpane," comprises an intertwined mermaid, merman, and dolphin riding on an ocean wave. Waugh's accomplished modeling of these elements points to his training as a sculptor, and the crisp outline of the symmetrical figures is further enhanced by the articulated lines of their musculature, and the stylized rendering of their hair, gesturing hands, and tails. In the case of the *Zodiac Bowl*, the beauty of the glass itself is less important than the decoration, which consists of "the twelve signs of the Zodiac circle on an upward diagonal," each figure "a complete composition, like a gem carved in light."[7] Like the figures on the punch bowl, Waugh's symbols of the Zodiac, including Taurus, Gemini, and Scorpio, produce an optical illusion: the copper-wheel engraving gives the decoration a raised effect. Moreover, the *Zodiac Bowl* is decidedly imitative of a charger known as *Vindrosen*, which was conceived by Swedish designer Edvard Hald and exhibited at The Metropolitan Museum of Art in 1936. Although the form and decoration of the Swedish piece—consisting of actively posed figures encircling the rim—are remarkably similar to the *Zodiac Bowl*, the latter exhibits a formal, more restrained quality; its figures are carefully and evenly spaced, while the former displays a more playful, asymmetrical scheme.[8] Having secured a reputation as the premier American producer of high-quality, modern glass, Steuben opened showrooms in Chicago and Palm Beach. The firm further popularized its designs in exhibitions such as one held at the Art Institute in 1938. This show, which gave Chicagoans their first substantial viewing of Steuben glass, included thirty pieces, seven of them designed by Waugh.[9] Described in the *Chicago Daily News* as a "mecca of society's art devotees," the display included a *Zodiac Bowl* identical to the Art Institute's, and this *Trident Punch Bowl*, which was purchased for the Art Institute's collection.[10]

The entrepreneurial Gates continued to pursue new possibilities for publicity and artistic innovation. In 1937, for example, he persuaded the French artist Henri Matisse to provide a sketch for engraving, and soon recruited twenty-six similarly renowned painters, printmakers, and sculptors to create decorative motifs for his company's glassware. The fruits of these efforts were displayed in the exhibit "Collection of Designs in Glass by Twenty-Seven Contemporary Artists," held at Steuben's New York showroom three years later.[11] The entries were produced in editions of six (increasing their exclusivity), and included work by Matisse, Giorgio de Chirico, Salvador Dali, André Derain, Raoul Dufy, Georgia O'Keeffe, Grant Wood, and the sculptor Paul Manship. Unlike many of his fellow artists, who chose to simply supply sketches that could be engraved on existing glass designs, Manship planned both the form and decoration of the Art Institute's vase. He, along with Dufy, was praised for his choice to decorate most of the object's surface—for "using the transparency instead of ignoring it."[12]

In his design, Manship—described by Steuben as "the exponent of the archaic coupled with the intensely modern"—chose to depict the courtship of a centaur and a satyr in three engraved vignettes; these can be seen with great clarity through the glass body, allowing the viewer to comprehend the design scheme from all sides. Such scenes reflected Manship's long interest in archaic Greek sculpture and mythology, which he pursued during his studies at the American Academy in Rome (1909–12), and regularly applied to his own bronze sculpture.[13] Gates was undoubtedly drawn to Manship's work because the sculptor, like Waugh, tempered his classical designs with an extreme, modern precision that did not detract from the technical virtuosity of the glass itself.

18. **Margret Craver**

(American; 1907–1991)

Bonbonnière, 1938

Wichita, Kansas

Silver and cloisonné enamel; h. 5.7 cm (2¼ in.)

x diam. (base) 13.4 cm (5¼ in.)

Stamped on bottom: *STERLING*; C

(within a scalloped circle)

Americana Fund, 1985.516

Like Peer Smed (see cat. no. 15), Margret Craver created handcrafted holloware and jewelry out of traditional materials such as sterling silver and enamel, but at the same time imbued her dynamic pieces with colorful, energetic patterns, and Art Deco–inspired ornament and forms. Trained in the Arts and Crafts tradition of metalsmithing, she believed that designers should execute their own work. In the 1930s, however, this was an increasingly difficult goal for a number of reasons. The

demand for silversmiths had waned because handmade silver pieces could be acquired by only a small, affluent group of consumers, and because designers most often created wares that were machine-made by large companies. Moreover, metal artists had fewer educational opportunities, resulting from the economic hardships of the Great Depression and the rise of the industrial-design profession, which made mass-produced domestic objects more commonplace.[1] Indeed, Craver's metalworking education at the University of Kansas in Wichita left much to be desired, and upon her graduation in 1929 she studied privately with a number of master craftsmen who taught her the fundamentals of silversmithing. More importantly, they instilled in her a devotion to the handmade object. One of her most influential teachers was Arthur Nevill Kirk of Detroit, an ecclesiastical metalworker who headed the metals workshop at the Cranbrook Academy of Art (see cat. no. 19) from 1929 to 1933, and trained Craver in holloware forging.[2]

In 1938, after modern Scandinavian decorative arts had gained a measure of international recognition (see cat. nos. 15 and 17), Craver traveled to Stockholm to study with the renowned modern silversmith Erik Fleming.[3] Influenced by the smooth surfaces, decorative flourishes, and exquisite handcraftsmanship of Fleming's work, Craver created the Art Institute's bonbonnière upon her return to the United States that same year. The piece's smooth, silver body is surmounted by a hand-hammered lid, in which Craver set a brilliant, colorful enamel medallion with Art Deco–style geometric decoration. Craver may have learned such enamel techniques from Kirk, whose work often incorporated colorful enamels.[4] The object's form, which also resembles round Art Deco shapes such as Gene Theobald's tea service (cat. no. 9), is extremely unified: its stepped body is composed of six graduated circles, and the double rings encircling the medallion echo the inverted-"V"-shaped elements that join the base to the body. Craver's strict adherence to geometry in this piece provides a striking contrast to Smed's naturalistically undulating compote and candelabra (cat. no. 15)—produced only four and five years earlier, respectively—and indicates the wide variety of modern stylistic influences present during the 1930s.

Despite the success of her work, Craver was alarmed by the increasingly mechanized state of the silver industry, and was determined to challenge contemporary notions that held the silversmith to be "no longer a virtuoso of techniques," but rather "an engineer in silver."[5] In 1944 she helped establish the non-profit Hospital Service Program, which taught therapeutic metalsmithing techniques to injured war veterans. Through this and other programs, Craver sought to preserve endangered traditions of handwork and craft, and ensure the continued vitality of American silversmithing.[6]

19. J. Robert F. Swanson, Pipsan Saarinen Swanson, and Eliel Saarinen

(American; 1900–1981)
(American, born Finland; 1905–1979)
(American, born Finland; 1873–1950)

Nesting Tables, 1939

Made by Johnson Furniture Company,
Grand Rapids, Michigan
Maple; largest table 45.7 x 76.2 x 47 cm (18 x 30 x 18½ in.)
Stamped on underside of smallest table:
Johnson-Handley-Johnson Co./Grand Rapids, Mich.
(in a circle); *FHA* (radiating from circle)
Promised gift of Suzanne Martyl Langsdorf

Part of the "Flexible Home Arrangements" (*FHA*) group of furniture designed in 1939 by J. Robert F. Swanson, his wife Pipsan Saarinen Swanson, and her father Eliel Saarinen, these nesting tables were created as a solution to the lack of affordable, modern furnishings available at the time. The three lightweight components, which are elegantly proportioned and fit compactly within one another, represent an early example of the flexible modular furniture popularized in America following World War II (see cat. no. 28); they could be used together or separately, and easily moved throughout the home. Functional and versatile, *FHA* was manufactured from 1939 onward by the Johnson Furniture Company, and included beds, chests-of-drawers, corner tables, nesting tables, and other pieces, all made from North Michigan birch or blond maple; some pieces featured painted-silver detailing. The neutral, light colors and spare decoration of the pieces allowed owners to use them in a variety of room settings and decorative schemes.[1]

Eliel Saarinen greatly influenced modern architecture and applied arts in the United States.[2] Like Frank Lloyd Wright (see cat. nos. 14, 27), Saarinen pursued an Arts and Crafts–based approach to unified interiors, and, to a large extent, disregarded historical precedent. Although he worked briefly in the Chicago area and taught architecture at the University of Michigan, it was through his work at the Cranbrook Academy of Art in Bloomfield Hills, Michigan, that Saarinen established himself as one of the most visible promoters of modern design in the United States.[3] Cranbrook was the inspiration of George Gough Booth, a Detroit newspaper magnate and philanthropist who hoped to establish an exceptional school and design community that

Figure 1

Hugo Henrik Alvar Aalto (Finnish; 1898–1976). *Armchair*, 1929/1933. Made by Artek, Helsinki, Finland. Bent and laminated birch; 57.5 x 61.3 x 87.6 cm (22 ⅝ x 24 ⅛ x 34 ½ in.). The Art Institute of Chicago, Cornelia Conger Endowment, restricted gift of Helen Johnson, restricted gift of Mrs. Joseph Regenstein by exchange, European Decorative Arts Purchase Fund (1983.601).

would train artists, and also serve as an atelier where students could create architecture and furnishings to improve the quality of American domestic life. By the mid-1930s, Booth had realized his dream: he hired Saarinen as the school's master architect around 1924, and together, they soon attracted a number of talented students and faculty, including Charles and Ray Eames and Maija Grotell (see cat. nos. 22, 24), whose work came to reflect the academy's atmosphere of intellectual innovation. Saarinen encouraged artistic collaboration—epitomized by his own family's work on the buildings' interiors—and nurtured a spirit of experimentation that led to the creation of some of the most inventive, technologically important designs of the twentieth century.[4]

In 1926, Saarinen's daughter Pipsan married one of her father's students, J. Robert F. Swanson. A student of ceramics, fabric design, metalwork, and weaving in Finland, Pipsan soon established a contemporary interior design department, considered one of the first of its kind, in her husband's architectural practice. The goal was to create interiors sympathetic to modern architecture, because, as Pipsan put it, the firm "found that *no* decorator in Detroit had the *slightest* idea what 'modern' was all about."[5] Likewise, the Swansons, together with Saarinen, created the *FHA* furniture line out of their frustration at the limited amount of affordable, well-designed, well-made modern furniture available to the average American consumer. Although not designed under the auspices of Cranbrook, *FHA* followed the academy's goals of integrating architecture, interiors, and furnishings, and blossomed from the school's emphasis on intellectual and artistic partnership. The line also represents a fusion of modernist idioms. Saarinen and the Swansons were partial to the contemporary, light-wood furniture produced in Finland by designers such as Alvar Aalto (fig. 1), and *FHA*'s warm, natural, wood finish echoes the blond materials employed in such Scandinavian designs.[6] Its forms were inspired more by the machine aesthetic, however; the Art Institute's rectilinear tables, for example, feature rounded, streamlined corners, and were also offered with a stainless-steel top.[7] Indeed, the manufacturer marketed the *FHA* line similarly to the affordable, modern metal furniture then being built by firms such as the Howell Company (see cat. no. 13).

The Shapes of Progress

Humanity, we are told, is on the verge of new things. Mankind is stirring and on the march. And ahead is a post-war world filled with prospects for the realization of man's fondest and oldest dreams. Among them is a good home to live in.

T. H. Robsjohn-Gibbings[1]

Following the turbulent years of the Depression era and World War II, Americans readied themselves for an age of progress and prosperity. The United States emerged from the war as the most wealthy and powerful nation in the world, and a heightened sense of patriotism became allied with the dream of home-ownership, often in the burgeoning suburbs. While the experience of the conflict shaped the needs and habits of postwar American consumers significantly—many were eager to progress beyond the devastating events of the past—the war also affected the ideas and aesthetics of modern design in substantial, exciting ways. While organically inspired objects remained popular, designers such as Samuel Marx and Edward Wormley developed custom furnishings that incorporated historicist elements and expensive materials both new and traditional (see cat. nos. 20–21). More important, however, were a number of technical innovations that emerged during the war and were soon adapted for domestic and commercial use. Largely due to the restrictions placed on combat-essential materials such as aluminum, chromium, copper, steel, and timber during war time, designers explored and experimented

with alternative substances, and, as a result, moved beyond previous stylistic boundaries. Charles and Ray Eames (see cat. no. 22) and Eero Saarinen (see cat. no. 29), for example, bent, stamped, and molded industrial materials such as plastics and plywood into imaginative furniture forms raised on bent-wood or steel rods. Through their efforts, these designers hoped to create high-quality furnishings that were imaginative yet standardized, and could be mass-produced for a large, middle-class audience who desired affordable, comfortable, and informal domestic objects. Furthermore, designers such as George Nelson revolutionized furniture placement and interior schemes by creating modular furnishings for families who owned smaller homes with fewer rooms and open floor plans (see cat. no. 28).

Believing that such home furnishings represented the most legitimate and democratic manifestations of modern design, the Museum of Modern Art, New York, was instrumental in marketing them to postwar consumers. The museum also offered itself as a forum in which designers could introduce forward-looking prototype designs;[2] MoMA also, as an article in the museum's *Bulletin* explained, "worked against the 'modernistic' and 'stream-line' fads which [had] so seriously perverted American design."[3] Through exhibitions such as the "International Competition for Low-Cost Furniture Design" (1948), the museum validated the experiments of designers such as the Eameses, stating: "To serve the needs of the vast majority of people we must have furniture that is planned for small houses and apartments, furniture that is well designed yet moderate in price, that is comfortable but not bulky, and that can be easily moved, stored, and cared for; in other words, mass-produced furniture that is integrated to the needs of modern living, production and merchandising."[4]

The popular "Good Design" exhibits (1950–55; fig. 1) were an integral part of MoMA's crusade to introduce affordable, high-quality modern design into American homes.[5] Initiated at the request of Chicago's Merchandise Mart, which sought to attract manufacturers of modern furnishings to the Midwest,[6] these displays aimed to "make the manufacturer, the buyer and the consumer more conscious of what constitutes good modern design and to promote it in a way that consumer demand will encourage the cautious buyer and the even less adventurous manufacturer."[7] Fabrics, floor coverings, furniture, household accessories, kitchenware, lamps, and tableware were included in the shows, and selected according to their "eye appeal, function, construction and price, with emphasis on the first."[8]

The "Good Design" exhibits were considered by many critics to be, like the streamlining trend of the 1930s, a marketing ploy: the program did, in fact, provide eye-catching, black-and-orange "tags, labels, ads, suggested window displays," and other paraphernalia to retailers—including department stores such as Bloomingdale Brothers, Abraham and Straus, and W. and J. Sloan—who sold "Good Design" in their establishments.[9] Nevertheless, the shows introduced audiences to the work of the Eameses, Wormley, and other designers, and promoted a progressive approach to design that, in its emphasis on simplified, functional forms, resembled the International Style principles which had taken root in the 1930s. Indeed, "Good Design" encompassed moral values as well as universal aesthetic qualities, and was necessarily affordable, mass produced, and available to a broad cross-section of American consumers.

The continuing influence of the Bauhaus designers was also revealed by numerous re-editions and reproductions of their work, beginning in the late 1940s. This resurgence sparked a revived interest in the anonymous,

Figure 3
"Designer Craftsmen,
U.S.A., 1953," The Art
Institute of Chicago,
Mar. 16–Apr. 26, 1954.

functional qualities of the International Style during the 1950s, which is seen in the spare silver designs of Arthur Pulos (see cat. no. 31), and the tubular-steel and leather furniture of William Katavolos, Douglas Kelley, and Ross Littell (fig. 2). In sharp contrast, however, handcrafted objects managed to maintain their popularity. Sustained by craft-based educational programs and exhibits including "Designer Craftsmen, U.S.A., 1953," held at the Art Institute in 1954 (fig. 3), craftspeople such as the ceramists Maija Grotell and Gertrud and

Otto Natzler, for example, used natural materials, their own labor, and traditional, often-unpredictable manufacturing processes to create unique works of art (see cat. no. 24).[10] In the face of a "disposable culture" that encouraged Americans to "keep up with the Joneses" by purchasing new homes, cars, and furnishings every few years,[11] such handmade objects—like the organic designs of the 1930s and 1940s—were seen to offer consumers a less standardized, more personal interpretation of modern design.

20. **Samuel A. Marx**

(American; 1885–1964)

Armchair, c. 1944

Made by William J. Quigley, Incorporated,
Chicago, Illinois
Birch, blond veneer, aluminum, and plastic;
77.1 x 55.8 x 45.2 cm (30³/₈ x 23¹/₈ x 17³/₄ in.)
Stamped beneath front seat rail: *QUIGLEY*
Gift of Mr. Leigh B. Block, 1981.179

Side Table, c. 1944

Chicago, Illinois
Painted pine and glass;
64.2 x 45.6 cm (25¹/₄ x 17 ¹⁵/₁₆ in.)
Gift of Mr. Leigh B. Block, 1981.174

In 1943, the prominent collectors and philanthropists Leigh and Mary Lasker Block commissioned the Chicago architect and designer Samuel A. Marx to design their lakefront apartment. For the residence, located at 1260 Astor Street on Chicago's Gold Coast, Marx custom-designed several pieces of furniture that not only complemented the Blocks' extensive art collection, but also embodied his own philosophy of modernism.[1] Like Edward Wormley (see cat. no. 21), Marx did not reject historical models in his architecture and furniture designs, but rather established his own modernist aesthetic by combining traditional cabinetmaking practices with sumptuous materials and inventive, reductive forms.

An avid collector of art in his own right, Marx graduated from the Massachusetts Institute of Technology with an architecture degree in 1907, and subsequently studied for two years at the Ecole des Beaux-Arts in Paris.[2] His work before 1933 is relatively obscure, but in that year he designed the first aluminum car for the Pullman Company, which was exhibited at the "Century of Progress International Exposition" in Chicago. This brief foray into industrial design seems not to have satisfied him, for he subsequently devoted his career to architecture, custom interiors, and furnishings.

The Art Institute's armchair and side table belong to a distinct genre of custom-made furniture designed by architects and interior designers—including Paul László, Tommi Parzinger, and T. H. Robsjohn-Gibbings— between the late 1930s and the early 1950s. Such designers did not strictly follow major modern trends such as streamlining or organicism, but instead drew upon neoclassicism, Art Deco, and even ancient influences.[3] This group of furniture designs displays refined proportions, unconventional materials, and playful interpretations of historicist forms. The style declined in popularity in the 1950s, when modern designers began, with new effectiveness, to exploit industrial materials in furniture intended for mass consumption.[4]

New construction slowed dramatically as a result of the Great Depression, and architects such as Marx turned to interior and furniture design for restaurants, hotels, shops, and offices; even before the crash, many business owners believed that making their spaces more efficient and modern would attract patrons.[5] The Chicago brokerage firm A. G. Becker & Company, for example, hired Marx to "modernize" its interiors in around 1928.[6] This type of custom work remained lucrative through World War II, and Marx continued to design interiors and coordinating furniture for commercial establishments such as the Pump Room restaurant in Chicago's Ambassador East Hotel (1938; fig. 1). In his redecoration of the original Georgian-style Pump Room, Marx incorporated neo-

Figure 1

Samuel A. Marx (American; 1885–1964). Pump Room restaurant at the Ambassador East Hotel, Chicago, Ill., c. 1940. Photo: *Architectural Record* 88, 1 (July 1940), p. 24.

classical elements such as dentil moldings and Palladian-style windows, while incorporating modern touches such as table lamps, low-intensity lighting, and deep-blue accents; as a writer for *Architectural Record* stated, "Mr. Marx's deceivingly simple scheme suggests that gracious design knows no style limitations."[7] In addition to his public commissions, Marx also attracted a devoted following of prestigious clients, including art collectors such as the Blocks, film star Edward G. Robinson, and department-store magnate Morton D. May.[8]

In 1945, *House Beautiful* remarked that

the Modern Movement is constantly torn between what Mr. Marx terms intellectualized design—sharp, radical, and functional—and an opposing inclination toward traditional forms and manners. Sensitive to both expressions, Mr. Marx . . . draws from both schools of thought. Pure Modernism he finds too naked and barren, too often lacking in quality. Pure traditionalism he finds outworn, repetitious, and dull. But his work is predominantly contemporary in that he employs a broad range of materials and is schemed to serve modern needs.[9]

Marx's range of materials did not, however, include Bauhaus-inspired glass and steel (see cat. nos. 12–13), or the molded plywood of his experimental contemporaries (see cat. no. 22). Influenced by the lavish designs of the Art Deco style, Marx instead favored luxurious textures and expensive materials such as *cracquelaire* lacquer, silver leaf, clear Lucite®, plexiglass, parchment and marbleized papers, shiny plastics, sharkskin, and light-wood veneers.[10] He envisioned his furniture as part of the structure of a room, as "one element of the whole, like a tile in a mosaic," and, like Eugene Schoen (see cat. no. 6), designed pieces only on a custom-order basis.[11] Because of the delicate nature of the materials that he worked with, as well as his attention to quality and the high standards of his well-to-do clientele, Marx did not rely upon machine production.[12] Instead, his designs were executed by the William J. Quigley Company of Chicago, a firm renowned for its fine cabinetmaking skills and reproductions of eighteenth-century French and English furniture.

Marx followed a dictum for contemporary interior design that linked the "skill of a decorator" to his or her ability to bring "the rugs, furniture, fabrics, and accessories into a harmonious unity, [while managing] to give the room enough variety so that it is constantly interesting."[13] Marx's furniture typically exhibits neutral tones and straight or gently curving lines, and is devoid of applied ornament; it was intended to complement antique furnishings, and did not compete with colorful works of art. The Art Institute's elegant side table was made as one of a pair intended for the Blocks' library (fig. 2), which the couple "furnished around a Van Gogh and a Soutine."[14] In this room Marx also included overstuffed upholstered chairs, heavy tassled drapes, and a table and two side chairs of his own conception. The side table's subtly organic form, composed of a three-part, pinwheel-shaped base with an open center and a corresponding glass top, suggests the contemporary fashion for biomorphic shapes. It defies conventional styling, however, and lacks the free-form contours and common materials used by designers such as Russel Wright (see cat. no. 16) and Charles and Ray Eames (see cat. no. 22). The light, undecorated surface suggests the appearance of marble, and the "spider-web lacquer" finish—which Marx produced with his *cracquelaire* technique—simulates the crazing, or fractured glaze, of Chinese ceramics.[15] Similarly, the Art Institute's dynamic armchair exhibits Marx's creative use of silhouettes and materials.[16] The cantilevered backrest floats surrealistically above the rounded seat, and is attached to curving, tubular-metal arms which recall elements of Bauhaus furniture designs by Marcel Breuer and Ludwig Mies Van der Rohe (see p. 49, fig. 2). Perhaps even more striking than the chair's design, however, is the dramatic contrast between the extremely light color of its frame and legs, and the stark, black plastic that covers the seat, back, and arms.

21. Edward Wormley

(American; 1907–1995)

Bench and Cushion, 1945/55

Probably New York, New York
Cherry, with stained plywood seat and
cotton/rayon cushion;
63.5 x 63.5 x 38.1 cm (25 x 25 x 15 in.)
Gift of Mr. and Mrs. Morris S. Weeden through
the Antiquarian Society, 2000.14

Like his better-known contemporaries Charles and Ray Eames (see cat. no. 22), George Nelson (see cat. no. 28), and Eero Saarinen (see cat. no. 29), Edward Wormley emphasized comfort, function, and simplicity in his furniture designs. Rather than striving to create anonymous or standardized forms, however, Wormley embraced the furniture designs of the past, adapting and manipulating them in order to create his own imaginative, distinctly American modern style. In his own words, "modern . . . is an expression of attitudes toward living and cannot be the same for everyone."[1] Wormley's furniture accommodated the needs of his clients, and, transcending design trends, blended easily into both modern and traditional interiors. Although the Art Institute's rare bench does not appear to have been included in any specific furniture line conceived by Wormley, its formal characteristics are sympathetic to the ideas of his "Janus Collection," which debuted in 1957. This line, according to contemporary publicity, was "appropriately named for the Roman god Janus who contemplates the future as well as the past. . . .[It] is distinguished by many features inspired by our design heritage yet is completely contemporary in its attention to convenience, scale, and comfort."[2]

Born in rural Illinois, Wormley had artistic aspirations that led him to Chicago, where he studied briefly at The School of the Art Institute. Although he showed significant promise as a student, financial constraints forced him to leave school after only three terms. He took a job in the interior design studio at Marshall Field and Company, where he helped design and furnish several lakefront apartments, and designed a line of eighteenth-century English reproduction furniture. Wormley's training at Field's provided him with valuable experience, and, at the age of twenty-three, he was hired as the first designer for Dunbar Furniture Corporation, a little-known manufacturer based in Berne, Indiana, which specialized in historically inspired furniture made from fine materials. Dunbar sought to upgrade its line of upholstered furniture, and Wormley soon convinced the company to add a number of modern pieces to its otherwise traditional offerings.[3] The great success of these items following World War II prompted the firm to concentrate exclusively on modern design.[4]

The popularity of Wormley's modern designs for Dunbar, which were sold in showrooms in major American cities from coast to coast, inspired him to open his own New York studio in 1944. There, he worked independently while retaining a professional relationship with Dunbar, and went on to produce some of the most creative designs of his career. He remained attentive to issues of ergonomics, proportion, and scale, and soon developed his own aesthetic vocabulary; he incorporated design elements of past furniture styles such as neoclassicism while emphasizing clean lines and function in order to create distinct forms. Wormley's approach to modern design was, for the most part, drastically different from those of his mid-century contemporaries. The 1950s saw a revival of the International Style, whose practitioners favored forms that were austere and undecorated. Wormley, however, resisted this ascetic impulse, as well as the common

Figure 1
Edward J. Wormley
(American; 1907–1995).
"Career Group" ensem-
ble. Photo: Dunbar
Furniture, *The Dunbar
Book of Contemporary
Furniture* (Berne, Ind.,
1953), p. 152.

modernist drive toward mass-produced stan-
dardization, and chose instead to maintain a
flexible, individual approach to interior design.
He was impressed by the metal furniture of
designers such as Ludwig Mies van der Rohe,
he later remembered, but "couldn't imagine [these] designs being used in a home and
thought they would find acceptance only in
hospitals."[5] At a time when other designers
favored innovative industrial materials such as
aluminum, plate glass, plastics, plywood, and
chrome-plated steel, Wormley stressed tradition and craftsmanship, and used exotic woods
and fine upholstery to create an "elegant contemporary [style], touched with intimacy,
warmth, and detail."[6] Although his ideas may
have differed from those of his peers, they were
heralded by newspapers and magazines seeking a style of modern design that their readers
could recognize and appreciate.[7] Wormley's
participation in the prestigious "Good Design"
exhibitions held from 1950 to 1955 at the Merchandise Mart in Chicago, and at the Museum
of Modern Art, New York (see p. 72), further
confirmed his critical success as a designer.

The Art Institute's bench epitomizes
Wormley's design intent. Its smooth, spare
form lacks ornament or decoration, which
emphasizes the warm, rich wood; the elegantly
sweeping sides are inspired by early nineteenth-
century neoclassical furniture. The bench
was one of a pair, and was originally part of
Wormley's own estate.[8] These pieces have not
been found in Dunbar Furniture catalogues or
advertisements, and it is probable that Wormley
created them for his own use, or custom-
designed them for one of his many devoted
patrons.[9] The benches' miniature size suggests
that they may each have been placed at the
end of a twin bed, like the "slipper benches"
in Wormley's "Career Group" (fig. 1).[10]

22. **Charles** and **Ray Eames**

(American; 1907–1978)

(American; 1912–1988)

Lounge Chair Wood (LCW), 1945/46

Made by Evans Products Company, Molded
Plywood Division, Venice, California, for Herman
Miller Furniture Company, Zeeland, Michigan
Molded and bent birch plywood, and rubber:
67.9 x 56.5 x 57.2 cm (26¾ x 22¼ x 22½ in.)
Paper label on bottom of seat: *Herman Miller/
Evans/Charles Eames*
Gift of Mrs. Eugene A. Davidson, 1970.1049

Folding Screen, 1946

Made by Evans Products Company, Molded
Plywood Division, Venice, California
Molded ash plywood and canvas:
172 x 150.1 x 8.2 cm (67¾ x 59⅛ x 3¼ in.)
Restricted gift of Marshall Field, 1981.5

Lounge Chair and Ottoman, 1956

Made by Herman Miller Furniture Company,
Zeeland, Michigan;Rosewood, leather, aluminum;
chair: 83.8 x 85.7 x 81.3 cm (33 x 33¾ x 32 in.)
ottoman: 62.9 x 43.2 x 54 cm (24¾ x 17 x 21¼ in.)
On bottom of chair seat: *Designed by Charles
Eames/Herman Miller/Zeeland, Mich.*
(circular metal plaque)
Gift of Mrs. Victor Figueroa, 2000.128.1–2

Charles and Ray Eames are regarded as one of the most influential design teams of the twentieth century; although it is Charles who has traditionally been given credit for the couple's extensive output, recent scholarship has brought attention to his wife's contributions, and their partnership is now recognized as a highly collaborative one.[1] The couple met in 1940 at the Cranbrook Academy of Art (see cat. no. 19), where Ray was a student and Charles served as head of the industrial-design department.[2] After marrying in 1941, they moved to Los Angeles and embarked on a design career that lasted over thirty years. Together, they not only designed furniture, but also created buildings, films, multimedia presentations, sculptures, and toys that reflect their interest in innovation, experimentation, and education.[3] The Art Institute's chairs and screen epitomize these interests, which point to the pair's Cranbrook roots. In addition, they symbolize the Eameses' desire to forge a new path in design, one that not only aimed to revolutionize the use of materials and construction following World War II, but hoped to change the shape of domestic life as well.

Attempting, like the Swansons (see cat. no. 19), to manufacture low-cost modern furniture for mass production, Charles began experimenting with inexpensive molded plywood at Cranbrook. There, he and colleague Eero Saarinen (see cat. no. 29)—undoubtedly inspired by the earlier bent-plywood furniture of Alvar Aalto (see cat. no. 19, fig. 1)—created entries for the landmark exhibition and competition entitled "Organic Design in Home Furnishings" (1940; see p. 49), sponsored by the Museum of Modern Art, New York. They won first prize for prototype chairs that were produced by molding wood into shapes with multiple curves contoured to fit the body.[4] After their move to California, the Eameses continued to experiment with molded-plywood technology in order to create high-quality, low-cost furniture. Although they were not the first designers to explore such techniques in the years between the two world wars, they were the first to use a single molding process to create plywood seats that curved in more than one direction. In 1941, the Eameses made prototype seats using their homemade "Kazam!" molding machine, and established the technique for making molded-plywood furniture that could be mass-produced for the postwar consumer.[5]

As a result of this technical breakthrough, Charles was hired under contract by the United States Navy to design leg and arm splints out of molded plywood for the war effort; they were eventually manufactured by the Molded Plywood Division of the Evans Products Company in Venice, California. Evans made aircraft and automobile parts during peacetime, and, impressed by the Eameses' developments with plywood, subsequently hired Charles to direct its research and development.[6] In 1945, with the end of the conflict in sight, Evans was ready, albeit hesitantly, to mass-produce furniture using the molded-plywood technology refined during the war. The company manufactured several of the Eameses' designs for molded chairs such as the Art Institute's *Lounge Chair Wood (LCW)*, and other forms such as the museum's folding screen. The Eameses' early work with Evans, and with each other, culminated in a 1946 exhibition at the Museum of Modern Art, entitled "New Furniture Designed by Charles Eames". The show included a selection of their all-plywood furniture, including *LCW* examples (some with upholstery), tables, and other designs made both wholly of plywood and from a combination of wood and metal materials.[7] In 1947, Charles Eames joined Herman Miller as a consultant, and in 1949 the company itself purchased the exclusive rights to manufacture, market, and distribute the Eameses' designs.

Like Russel Wright in the 1930s, the Eameses used their work to promote an aesthetic of relaxed, unceremonious living. Indeed, they and their publicists at Herman Miller believed that modern furniture styles and informality were intimately linked. The Art Institute's lightweight *LCW* was designed for relaxation, and could be easily moved from room to room according to the owner's needs; in fact, since the chairs incorporated "resin-impregnated wood surfaces," they could even be placed outdoors.[8] The *LCW* consists of five pieces of molded-and-bent plywood: seat, back, structural "spine" element, and two pieces that comprise the front and rear legs. The seat and back, which were molded to accommodate the sitter, are glued to the frame with inconspicuous rubber shock mounts, which enhance the frame's resilience, and eliminated the need for extra materials that would have interfered with the design. Made first by Evans and then by Herman Miller, the *LCW* was shown at the

1946 MoMA exhibit, where it was extolled as "[coming] closer to using the advantages of modern American production techniques for the benefit of the purchaser—in regard to comfort, quality and price—than any design thus far shown publicly."[9] The folding screen, made of curvilinear pieces of ash plywood connected by canvas joints, could also be readily moved because it could be neatly and compactly folded together to a width of nine and one-half inches. Conceived during the Eameses' early plywood experiments, the eight molded, "U"-shaped elements allow the screen to stand on its own, and give the piece an undulating, organic appearance. Offered in different heights, it could be used to casually separate one section of a room from another in the new, open floor plans of postwar American homes.

The couple's 1956 *Lounge Chair and Ottoman* was the final expression of their innovative work in molded wood. Charles Eames hoped that the ensemble, which has been referred to as a twentieth-century interpretation of the nineteenth-century English club chair, would have the "warm receptive look of a well-used first baseman's mitt."[10] In these pieces, the Eameses diverged from their typical philosophy of designing for affordable mass production: composed of polished aluminum, sumptuous leather, and four pieces of molded rosewood, this was their best-selling, as well as most expensive, creation.[11] It was also their most comfortable: a star-shaped aluminum base allowed the user to control the chair's angle and position, and cast-aluminum connectors were employed to join the tufted headrest, back, and seat, rendering the chair more flexible than the Eameses' earlier designs.

Although the partners used technology similar to that of their earlier, molded-wood furniture, such comfort features required hand as well as machine labor to produce, and added significantly to the pieces' cost. Despite their apparent complexity, however, both chair and ottoman could be put together or taken apart with a screwdriver. Still manufactured by Herman Miller today, the ensemble has remained popular into the twenty-first century both for its modern design and for its comfort and ease of motion. The thronelike lounge chair represented comfort and status in its own age, and continues to do so in ours: even as it appeals to contemporary consumers as an iconic symbol of postwar culture, it embodies the almost aggressive approach to relaxation and informality that prevailed in the prosperous 1950s.

Opposite page, below:

Figure 1

"Museum" table service, shown at "Modern China by Eva Zeisel," the Museum of Modern Art, New York, Apr. 1946. Photo: *Bulletin of The Museum of Modern Art* 14 (fall 1946), p. 10.

23. Eva Zeisel

(American, born Hungary; born 1906)

"Museum" Coffeepot, designed 1942/43

Made by Shenago Pottery Company for Castleton China, New Castle, Pennsylvania
Porcelain: 25.7 x 19.7 x 12.7 cm (10$\frac{1}{8}$ x 7$\frac{3}{4}$ x 5 in.)
Mr. and Mrs. Manfred Steinfeld Fund, 1999.295

Celebrated as the "preeminent designer of mass-produced American ceramics in the twentieth century," Eva Zeisel regularly combines whimsical and ergonomic shapes, organically undulating lines, and clean, unadorned surfaces in her work.[1] Her "Museum" coffeepot, part of a twenty-five-piece table service (fig. 1), presents an elegant interpretation of modernism while at the same time retaining a traditional, recognizable form.[2] "The first fine china of modern design to be manufactured in this country," the "Museum" line represented a remarkable achievement for World War II–era domestic ceramics in terms of its materials and refined aesthetics.[3] Although several groups of modern earthenware were manufactured in the 1930s, including Frederick Hurten Rhead's "Fiesta Ware" (1935) and Russel Wright's "American Modern" (1937; see cat. no. 16), Zeisel's "Museum" service was the first modern, formal dinnerware service to be executed in porcelain. Indeed, the soft, ivory hue of the service's sophisticated vessels alludes to their fine material, and marks a distinct departure from the fanciful, brightly colored ceramics popularized in the 1930s.

In 1938, after working as a ceramic designer in Hungary, Germany, and Russia for over fifteen years, Zeisel settled permanently in New

York, and began teaching at the Pratt Institute, Brooklyn, and the Rhode Island School of Design, Providence, while designing ceramic wares for various companies. For example, she designed earthenware lines such as "Town and Country" for the Red Wing Pottery of Red Wing, Minnesota (1945), and "Tomorrow's Classic" for the Hall China Company of East Liverpool, Ohio (1949/50; fig. 2).[4] It was her association with the newly formed Castleton China Company, however, that gained Zeisel's ceramics critical recognition and national prestige. Aware of the role of New York's Museum of Modern Art as a liaison between industry and consumers—it sponsored competitions and exhibitions such as "Organic Design in Home Furnishings" (1940; see p. 49)—Castleton enlisted the help of Eliot Noyes, director of the museum's industrial-design department, to recruit an artist "to evolve a fine modern shape for formal dinnerware of high quality."[5] The chosen designer's wares would be manufactured by Shenago Pottery Company, a Castleton subsidiary, and displayed in a solo exhibition at MoMA. Dedicated to promoting objects void of "unnecessary" ornament, Noyes recommended Zeisel, whose work emphasized functional qualities such as balance and simplicity.

Zeisel's pattern fulfilled Noyes's criteria for good design, and also appealed to the American public. Although the coffeepot's traditional form and smooth surfaces evoke a sense of refinement and Bauhaus-inspired austerity, its softly curving contours allude to the organically inspired designs that became popular in the 1930s and 1940s. The Art Institute's piece illustrates Zeisel's conception for the service: "I wanted to design a service of real elegance. . . . That's why I gave the pieces an erect, uplifted look, as if they were growing up from the table."[6] The pot's slender neck swells out to form a bulbous middle, which tapers toward the bottom. The arching spout appears to

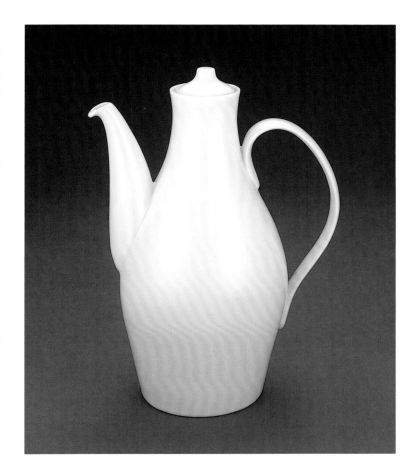

emerge from the body, its gently tipped rim suggesting the head of a small bird; the handle gracefully extends to accommodate a hand.

The "Museum" service's public premiere at the Museum of Modern Art in April 1946, only months after the acclaimed Charles Eames furniture exhibit (see cat. no. 22), was the museum's first solo presentation of a female designer's work. Although the Art Institute's coffeepot displays the subtle inspiration of contemporary organic design, it exhibits the timeless modernity that Castleton hoped for when it commissioned Zeisel's work. As the designer later recalled, "Castleton's 'Museum' shape was supposed to be a modern shape, acceptable to the advocates of the Modern Movement, but also to the elegant, sophisticated rich who could afford it; it had to be stately and formal, simple and elegant, fit to become an 'heirloom.'"[7]

Figure 2
Eva Zeisel (American, born Hungary; born 1906). *Platter*, c. 1953. Made by Hall China Company (East Liverpool, Oh.). Porcelain; 5.2 x 43.5 x 27.9 cm (2 x 17⅛ x 11). The Art Institute of Chicago, gift of Vera Ann Ciciora (1991.435).

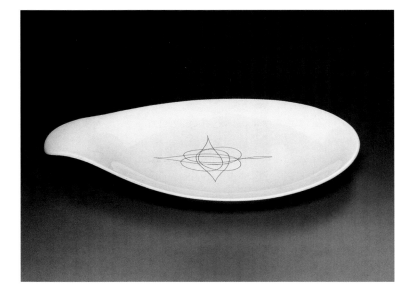

24. Maija Grotell

(American, born Finland; 1899–1973)

Vessel, c. 1946

Bloomfield Hills, Michigan
Glazed stoneware; h. 18.4 cm (7¼ in.) x diam. (top) 7.6 cm (3 in.) x diam. (base) 10.1 cm (4 in.)
Incised on base: *M G*, in script
Bequest of Russell Tyson, 1964.527

Gertrud and Otto Natzler

(American, born Austria; 1908–1971)
(American, born Austria; born 1908)

"Coupe," or Footed Bowl, 1945/46

Los Angeles, California
Glazed earthenware; h. 6 cm (2⅜ in.) x diam. (top) 19.1 cm (7½ in.) x diam. (base) 3.5 cm x (1⅜ in.)
Hand lettered on base: *NATZLER* (in black block letters)
Atlan Ceramic Club Fund, 1946.268

Teardrop Bottle with "Tigereye" Reduction Glaze, 1963

Los Angeles, California
Glazed earthenware; h. 25.1 cm (9⅞ in.)
Hand lettered on base: *NATZLER* (in black block letters); paper label on base: *M 633*
Restricted gift of Mrs. Francis Clow Thayer Alschuler Philanthropic Fund, and Mary Louise Womer, 1963.1162

The ceramics of Maija Grotell and of Gertrud and Otto Natzler sprang from Arts and Crafts traditions that embraced the handmade object. Extremely experimental in their art, all three ceramists worked within a studio environment, devoting their careers to discovering new clay formulas, body proportions, and glaze techniques. Moreover, they designed, created, fired, and embellished their own wares, rather than relying upon a manufacturer to make and distribute them. Like Charles Fergus Binns and Adelaide Alsop Robineau before them (see cat. no. 4), they were committed to making vessel forms intended for aesthetic enjoyment rather than daily use. Drawing upon both Chinese and Scandinavian influences, as well as the natural world around them, Grotell and the Natzlers created technically adventurous ceramics not unlike those made by Binns and his students at Alfred University earlier in the century. In their experimental approach and passionate dedication

to their medium, however, they also resembled contemporary furniture designers such as Charles and Ray Eames (see cat. no. 22) and Eero Saarinen (see cat. no. 29).

Mid-twentieth-century handmade ceramics are often rather subdued in shape and color, possibly in reaction to the whimsical, casual wares designed by artists such as Russel Wright that were mass-produced in the 1930s (see cat. no. 16)—or perhaps due in part to World War II, which made it difficult for potters to obtain ingredients such as uranium, which was used to create orange glaze.[1] Many of these pieces rely for their success on their maker's technical skill and refined aesthetic sense. Otto Natzler, for instance, wrote that American ceramics at that time were inspired by the "Sung period of China—the zenith of ceramic art—whose potters had the great wisdom and knowledge of their medium and who also used good taste and restraint in applying this knowledge to their work."[2] Furthermore, many ceramists

labored in artistic and educational environments that fostered a studio atmosphere in which teacher and student worked closely together to produce imaginative, and often original, results. Grotell, for example, was extremely influential in establishing a formal ceramics program at the Cranbrook Academy of Art (see cat. no. 19).

Born and educated in Helsinki, Finland, where she studied ceramics, design, painting, and sculpture, Grotell was briefly employed as a textile designer before immigrating to New York City in 1927. She studied with Binns at Alfred University, and later worked as a ceramics instructor at several studios and settlement houses before 1938, when she was hired by fellow Finnish émigré Eliel Saarinen (see cat. no. 19) at Cranbrook.[3] Cranbrook proved a suitable match for Grotell, in part because its cooperative, craft-oriented artistic atmosphere freed her from the necessity of making ceramics for industrial production.[4]

Grotell was a decorated potter before arriving in Bloomfield Hills.[5] Although her primary role at Cranbrook was as a teacher—she inspired the work of students such as Toshiko Takaezu (see fig. 1)—she created a number of her own stoneware pieces. While her early works were more decorative, sometimes incorporating vivid colors and pictorial scenes, the objects she made at Cranbrook emphasize surface texture, and illustrate her commitment to large, cylindrical or globular stoneware vessels that she threw on a wheel and fired at an extremely high temperature.[6] Cranbrook's environment encouraged her to experiment with color and a variety of glaze techniques; she often used matte glazes, Chinese-inspired wood-ash glazes, and the *pâte-sur-pâte* method—seen on the Art Institute's vase—which involves painting a clay body with layers of slip (liquid clay) to enhance the play of light and shade on the surface of a piece.

The Art Institute's vessel is a splendid example of Grotell's oeuvre. A virtual sphere, its bold, simple form lacks any carved or applied decoration. Nonetheless, the subtle rings around the vessel—which Grotell created on the wheel—exhibit an extremely tactile quality. The potter overlaid the vessel's pale-gray, stonelike surface with an irregular, sheer-white pattern of rings that encircles the body and suggests feathers, adding to the object's visual texture. Purchased from the "Modern Ceramics and Woodenware" exhibition held at the Art Institute in 1946, this vessel was one of the pieces by Grotell that, according to the *Chicago Tribune*, possessed a "massive, monumental quality," and displayed "dull, nature tones of wood-brown and granite-gray that enhance this simple, almost rustic feeling."[7]

Although the artist avoided mass production, and did not attempt to duplicate any of her pieces exactly, she often repeated a design in order to perfect it. For example, she displayed a piece remarkably similar to the Art Institute's (1952/53; Detroit Institute of Arts) in the "Designer Craftsmen, U.S.A., 1953" exhibition held at the museum in 1954 (see p. 73). This show, according to the exhibition catalogue, revealed in American ceramics "innumerable points of view, and a wide diversity of approach; stemming not from a single 'cultural root,' but from the myriad cultural roots that serve as a background in our huge American melting pot."[8] Indeed, the Scandinavian handicraft tradition that had established itself in the United States in the 1920s remained influential through the 1940s, and undoubtedly influenced the elegant glaze combinations and modern decoration of Grotell's ceramics.

Although Gertrud and Otto Natzler neither studied nor taught at Cranbrook, their partnership in many ways resembled the collaborative efforts the academy fostered so successfully. Gertrud created the forms of their low-fired earthenware pieces, while her husband, Otto, formulated and applied the dramatic glazes; together, they crafted one-of-a-kind wares until Gertrud's death in 1971.[9] Born and educated in Vienna, the Natzlers began their careers as ceramists in the early 1930s. Around 1935, Gertrud attempted to perfect delicately thin, classical forms, and Otto experimented with temperamental glaze recipes and firing techniques. Their combined efforts resulted in a recognizably individual style quite unlike the colorful, ceramic sculpture being produced in Vienna by the Wiener Werkstätte, and in the United States as well.[10] Their increasingly close working relationship culminated in several early successes for the largely self-taught couple, including a silver medal for their entries at the 1937 "Exposition internationale" in Paris. The following year, the couple married, and immigrated to Los Angeles to escape religious persecution and growing political instability in their homeland; both of the Natzlers were Jewish.[11]

Los Angeles offered them the artistic freedom and rich natural resources they needed in order to continue their ceramics experiments. California studio-pottery traditions

Figure 1

Toshiko Takaezu (American; born 1922). *Ka-hua Skidmore White*, 1990. Glazed stoneware; 142.2 x 78.7 cm (56 x 31 in.). The Art Institute of Chicago, gift of Lenore Tawney (1996.671).

were strong, and an active community of modern artists included other Austrian émigrés, among them the architect and designer Richard Neutra (see cat. no. 14). Using the state's indigenous red clays—often visible at the bases of their works—the Natzlers created numerous variations of traditional bowls, bottles, spheres, and vases that, as one critic described them, "defy duplication." Employing colorful, textural glazes adorned with names such as "Velvet Chartreuse," "Seaweed Jade," and "Green Pompeian Lava," Otto mastered a number of decorative characteristics—including burn or smoke marks, craters, color mutations, and fissures created in the kiln—that he was able to produce through unpredictable firing techniques.[12]

The Art Institute's pieces represent the finest of the Natzlers' creations. The eggshell-thin turquoise coupe—reminiscent of work from China's Northern Song Dynasty (960–1127)—is exquisitely rendered; the shallow, flaring bowl is supported by a small, yet elegantly proportioned, foot. The bowl itself appears to have been dipped into brilliant blue glaze, which covers the entire piece except for a small section of red earthenware visible on the foot. The piece's thin, red rim echoes this clay, and an allover sprinkling of semi-iridescent red-bronze flecks, achieved in the kiln, lends the object a textured appearance. Purchased by the Art Institute for thirty-five dollars from its "Modern Ceramics and Woodenware" exhibit of 1946, the coupe, with its simple, graceful form, exemplifies the way in which the Natzlers' pottery can, as one contemporary critic put it, complement "with singular felicity the clean-cut austerity of good modern furnishings."[13] The couple's dignified *Teardrop Bottle*, which the Art Institute bought from its own, monumental exhibition of their work in 1963, epitomizes the harmonious synthesis between form and glaze that the Natzlers so often achieved.[14] The brown, smoky-gray,

and mottled-yellow "tigereye" glaze fuses with the graceful form of the body, which Otto described as one that "ascends slowly upward with a slight curve, as if turning onto itself, only to change direction faintly just before ending."[15]

25. Attributed to Oscar Riedener
(American, born Switzerland; born 1911)

Pitcher, 1947/56
Made by Tiffany and Company, New York, New York
Silver; 28.3 x 20.3 x 14 cm (11 1/8 x 8 x 5 1/2 in.)
Marked on bottom: *Tiffany & Co./Makers/Sterling Silver/12673w*
The Orbit Fund, 1999.292

Since the last quarter of the nineteenth century, Tiffany and Company, founded in 1837 by Charles Louis Tiffany and John B. Young as a "fancy articles and curiosities shop," has been internationally renowned as a maker of handmade artistic silver wares, including jewelry, presentation pieces, and articles for domestic use. The firm created Japanese- and Islamic-inspired designs and mixed metal wares in response to the burgeoning taste for exoticism in the 1870s and 1880s, and popularized its colonial-revival and Art Nouveau–style silver in the 1880s and 1890s.[1] Tiffany's output of domestic wares during the first half of the twentieth century is somewhat obscure, however, perhaps due to two world wars and a national depression that interrupted the firm's design and production efforts. The Art Institute's pitcher survives as a rare example of Tiffany's mid-century, modernist creations, and suggests how the company experimented with contemporary design trends while retaining its focus on handmade luxury wares.

During World War I, Tiffany volunteered its facilities and skilled craftsmen to the manufacture of surgical instruments, and presentation pieces for distinguished military service. Soon afterward, the firm made silver in the Art Moderne, or Art Deco, style. The fashion for Art Deco silver waned by 1940, however, and the onset of World War II required Tiffany to once again adapt itself to a climate of conflict. In 1947, the United States War Production Board issued a statement describing silver's utility to the war effort, and asked civilians to "refrain from seeking products made of silver." Since silver conducts electricity as well as copper, of which there was a shortage, silver was substituted for copper in many cases so that the latter could be saved for "vital military applications."[2] The fashioning of luxury silver items therefore ceased, and the Tiffany factory was converted for the production of aircraft engine parts for both the army and navy.[3]

In the prosperous years following the war's end, a widespread interest in affordable "good design" was combined with both a resurgence of the standardized, industrial International Style, and a renewed fervor surrounding the traditional materials and craft ideals promulgated by designers such as Maija Grotell and Gertrud and Otto Natzler (see cat. no. 24). These philosophies often coalesced in objects such as the Art Institute's silver pitcher. Made under the direction of Oscar Riedener, Tiffany and Company's President of Design,[4] this piece was most likely custom made, and personifies the tradition of quality handwork that is inextricably associated with the firm. Like "neofunctionalist" silver pieces such as those of Arthur Pulos and William Frederick (see cat. no. 31), the pitcher is devoid of historical references, and exemplifies the sleek, unadorned, modern design idiom that is typically associated with machine manufacture. The hammered texture of the body, however, recalls

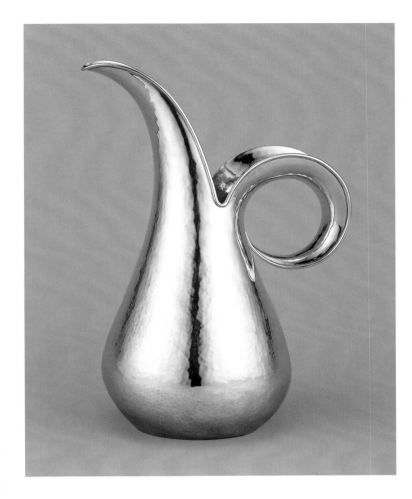

the handcrafted aesthetic of American Arts and Crafts metalwork, and the biomorphic form intimates the influence of abstract organicism that began in the 1930s with objects such as Russel Wright's woodenware and ceramics (see cat. no. 16), and continued following World War II. Emerging from a bulbous body that tapers at the neck, the arching spout and curving handle suggest a split botanical stalk that splays in two directions to create a dynamic, and unexpected, form.

26. **Henry P. Glass**
(American, born Austria; born 1911)

"Swingline" Child's Wardrobe, 1952
Made by Fleetwood Furniture Company,
Grand Haven, Michigan
Painted Masonite® and wood; 107.6 x 80.7 x 44.5 cm
(42³/₈ x 31³/₄ x 17¹/₂ in.)
Gift of Henry P. Glass, 2000.133

Coffee Service, 1954
Made by Plateria de Taxco, Taxco, Mexico
Silver and rosewood; coffeepot: 33 x 11.4 x 11.4 cm
(13 x 4¹/₂ x 4¹/₂ in.)
sugar bowl and cream pitcher: 7.6 x 10.2 x 10.2 cm
(3 x 4 x 4 in.)
Promised gift of Anne Karin Glass, daughter
of the artist

In his 1996 treatise entitled *The Shape of Manmade Things*, Henry Glass stated that "good design is governed by indisputable rules, unalterable by conditions of historic environment or location."[1] Indeed, his own designs for furniture and silver defy historical inspiration, and emphasize originality, function, and "honest" materials that are presented for what they are rather than being disguised as something else. Trained as an architect in his native Vienna, Glass immigrated to New York in 1939, and worked for several of the city's foremost designers and architects, including Gilbert Rohde. In 1942, he relocated to Chicago, and in 1945 formed his own firm, Henry P. Glass Associates, which specialized in "problem solving for industry." Glass's firm completed many inventive architectural and design jobs, including the Kling Photographic and Art Studios in Chicago (1946) and the Condado Beach Hotel in San Juan, Puerto Rico (1949).[2]

Glass also created modern, highly functional designs for adult and juvenile domestic furniture, institutional and office interiors, and household products, including clocks and lighting fixtures.[3] He was not only an active designer, but emerged as a teacher and passionate writer on the subject of modern design. In 1945, he initiated the first industrial-design program at The School of the Art Institute of Chicago, and served as professor there from 1946 until 1968. At the School, he promoted his fundamental design philosophy by lecturing on subjects such as structure, proportion, color, rhythm, and symmetry, and by publishing numerous studies of modern architecture and design, and of his various projects.[4]

Glass's award winning designs for durable and lightweight furniture, including modular pieces, could be inexpensively mass-produced for increasingly mobile postwar families.[5] Like Charles and Ray Eames (see cat. no. 22) and

Eero Saarinen (see cat. no. 29), Glass took advantage of the new materials and production techniques—Masonite®, plastics, and molded plywood, to name a few—that emerged during the 1920s, 1930s, and 1940s. Along with his contemporaries, Glass was highly concerned with economical design, and the affordability of Masonite®, as well as its malleable qualities and its ability to withstand everyday use by children, drew Glass to this product in particular.[6] His attention to color, and to simple, functional forms such as the Art Institute's wardrobe, therefore, appealed to American consumers while providing them with practical, well-designed furnishings for their children's rooms.

His highly successful "Swingline" group (1952), which consisted of beds, bookshelves, cabinets, desks, and other pieces, met with critical acclaim—it won the Industrial Design Institute's Gold Medal Award in 1952—and pioneered the use of Masonite® as a structural material for modular furniture. The Art Institute's painted-Masonite® wardrobe displays the bold, contrasting colors favored by 1950s consumers, and testifies to Glass's talent for imaginative, utilitarian design. Intended to appeal to young users, the wardrobe's blocky compartments of vivid blue, orange, red, and yellow also helped children organize their belongings. Long handles and small holes, for example, allowed little hands to open the molded bins and seats easily. Like the *Eames Storage Units (ESU)* designed by the Eameses in 1950, this piece—and "Swingline" furniture in general—was constructed of standardized, interchangeable Masonite® panels, and exhibits a "knock-down" aesthetic emphasizing ready disassembly and easy portability.[7] While the wardrobe's visible nail heads allude to its construction, many other "Swingline" products had tubular legs that owners could detach as needed.

Although Glass most often used "contemporary methods and techniques to satisfy contemporary requirements of function, aesthetics, and economy," he also designed several sterling-silver and rosewood ensembles, such as the Art Institute's coffee service.[8] Since he did not typically work in sumptuous materials, this elegantly simplified piece, consisting of a slender coffeepot, a sugar bowl, and a cream pitcher nestled into a serving tray, is a rare example in his oeuvre. The coffeepot's tall, rectilinear body tapers where the handle is attached, and flares out slightly to accommodate the subtly concave top, surmounted by a rosewood finial. Glass echoed the severe angle of the handle in the spout, and repeated both the handle and finial designs in the cream and sugar accessories. A unique ensemble—it was made for the artist's wife—the set further exhibits Glass's attention to shape and proportion, and its exceptionally modern look presents a superbly innovative revision of traditional silver design.

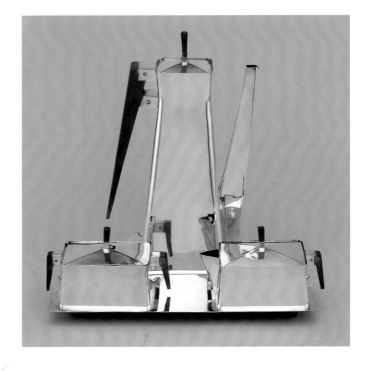

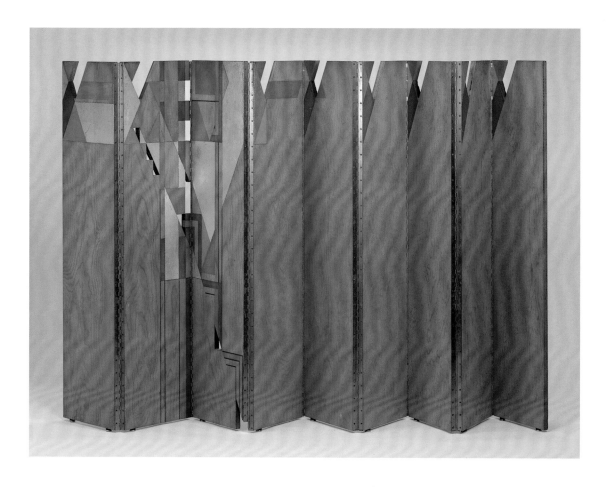

27. **Frank Lloyd Wright**

Screen, c. 1953

Painting executed by Eugene Masselink
(American, born South Africa; 1910–1962)
Painted plywood; 137.1 x 320 x 1.9 cm
(54 x 126 x 3/4 in.)
Gift of Mr. and Mrs. Thomas E. Keys, 1985.8

Like the screen designed by Charles and Ray Eames (see cat. no. 22), Frank Lloyd Wright's nine-paneled plywood partition was intended to offer privacy in a postwar home with an open floor plan. Custom-made rather than mass-produced, Wright's screen was conceived for the house that he designed for Mr. and Mrs. Thomas E. Keys in Rochester, Minnesota.[1] In its original setting, the screen served to divide the kitchen and dining space, adding a dynamic feature to a house in which the kitchen, living, and dining areas essentially functioned as one great, open room (fig. 1).[2] Although Wright's screen utilizes the simple material that Charles and Ray Eames favored in their molded-wood experiments during the 1940s (see cat. no. 22), it does not incorporate any inventive technological features; it consists merely of cut-and-painted plywood boards connected by brass hinges. Like his much earlier, geometrically informed furniture for the Imperial Hotel in Tokyo, Wright's screen emphasizes sharp lines and angular voids, and suggests his own distinctive approach to modern design.[3]

Whenever possible, Wright insisted on designing furniture for his buildings because he believed that "very few of the houses were anything but painful . . . after the clients brought in their own belongings."[4] The surroundings of the home itself continued to comprise an important element of his designs; according to the architect, the "new" style of the Keyses' cement-block, pine, and plate-glass "berm-house," so-called because of its setting on a narrow, hillside ledge, "began to associate with the ground and became natural to its prairie site."[5] Furthermore, Wright spoke of a "new freedom" in the elimination of doors and separate rooms, as he considered open domestic spaces more livable than "cellular sequestrations."[6] Wright designed some furniture for the Keys house, including several built-in cabinets and shelves, but did not conceive of the painted screen as part of the original furnishings. In 1952, about a year after moving into the house, Mrs. Keys approached Wright about designing a partition to disguise her activities in the kitchen. Wright was not keen on the idea, and instructed Allen Davidson, a Taliesen fellow who had supervised the house's construction, to reply that "[Mr. Wright] wishes you would try to live in the house for awhile without a screen [because he] says it takes time to adjust yourself to living this new way. He plans to visit you in the Spring [and] says if you still want the kitchen shut off that he will give you something more appropriate at the time."[7]

Wright ultimately designed the screen despite his reservations, and commissioned Eugene Masselink to paint its bold decorations. In addition to serving as Wright's secretary beginning in 1933, Masselink was often hired to paint murals and wall panels for buildings designed by Wright and other architects.[8] The Art Institute's screen is representative of Wright's philosophy of decoration for an "organic" home such as the Keyses'. He felt that "when you gloss [an object] over, lose its nature—enamel it, and so change the character of its natural expression, you have committed a violation according to the ideals of organic architecture."[9] In making furniture, Wright used "nothing applied which tends to eliminate the true character of what is beneath, or which may become substitute for whatever that may be."[10] Indeed, it was Wright's intention to allow the plywood's natural quality to equal the vivid red, blue, brown, and gold geometric shapes; the unpainted sections are not heavily stained or varnished, which allows the figure of the wood to resonate as part of the screen's decoration.

Figure 1

Interior of Mr. and Mrs. Thomas E. Keys Residence, Rochester, Minn., c. 1950–51. Photo: *Northwest Architect* 33, 5 (July/Aug. 1969), p. 35.

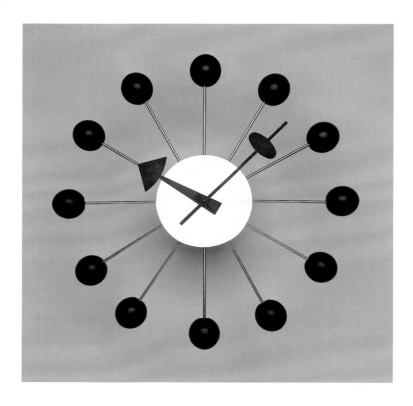

28. **George Nelson**
(American; 1908–1986)

Ball Clock, 1949
Made by Howard Miller Clock Company,
Zeeland, Michigan
Chrome-plated and black-enameled metal,
ebonized wood; diam. 34.3 cm (13½ in.)
Label on reverse: *howard miller clock
company/ZEELAND, MICHIGAN/115 V. 60 CY.
2 WATTS*
Orbit Fund, 1999.678

Coconut Chair, 1955
Made by Herman Miller Furniture Company,
Zeeland, Michigan
Fiberglass, aluminum, nylon and chlorofiber
upholstery; 85.1 x 40 x 86.4 cm (33½ x 40 x 34 in.)
Gift of Malcom, Kay, Kim, and Kyle Kamin, 1986.35

George Nelson's whimsical *Ball Clock* and *Coconut Chair* exemplify their designer's belief that even modern American furniture and domestic accessories were steeped in the "American tradition." Like antique pieces, Nelson thought, modern furnishings were necessarily the result of the materials, technology, and culture of their time.[1] Constructed of industrial materials such as aluminum, fiberglass, and chrome-plated metal, the pieces transform two recognizable shapes and symbols— the atom and the coconut—into objects for everyday use.

Nelson was one of the most prominent designers of furniture, lighting fixtures, and decorative accessories from the 1940s to the 1960s. A practicing architect, he began to write about industrial design during the 1930s, when the field was rapidly expanding despite the depressed national economy. In the February 1934 issue of *Fortune*, for example, he proclaimed that even the "formerly art-less industries"—producers of appliances, automobiles, electrical machinery, and other goods—were beginning to employ designers. Design, he predicted, was "certainly here to stay in a number of industries that knew it not before."[2]

Coupled with his own architectural projects, Nelson's research for articles, and for the book *Tomorrow's House: A Complete Guide for the Home Builder* (1945), tackled design issues such as storage, and the placement of furniture in the more open spaces of postwar homes. His built-in *Storagewall* of 1944 (fig. 1), conceived with *Tomorrow's House* coauthor Henry Wright, not only revolutionized the way Americans thought of closet and storage space, but also responded to the heightened pace of postwar consumerism. Part wall and part cupboard, drawer, and shelving system, the *Storagewall* accommodated the "junk and useful articles" of the average homeowner without taking up the space of a closet, and was celebrated as "a new answer to the housewife's demand for better storage."[3]

Following on the *Storagewall*'s success, Nelson entered into a long and productive consulting relationship with the Herman Miller Furniture Company. Nelson created both furniture and graphic designs during his twenty years with the firm, for which he also recruited influential designers such as Charles and Ray Eames (see cat. no. 22) and Isamu Noguchi. Nelson's first furniture line for Herman Miller drew upon his space-saving concept for the *Storagewall* in that owners could use pieces interchangeably—in different rooms, and in a number of ways. Nelson's famous slat bench, the foundation of this modular line, could be used as extra seating, as a coffee table, or as a base for storage cabinets and cubes.[4]

In 1947, Nelson established his own architectural and design office in New York City,

continuing to serve as a consultant to Herman Miller. The Art Institute's *Ball Clock*, which Nelson designed for the Howard Miller Clock Company, belongs to his "Chronopak" series of electric clocks, which was marketed to "the interior designer who doesn't want any eighteenth or nineteenth century faces in his twentieth-century interiors."[5] Each "Chronopak" clock exhibits a colorful or playful form that reduces time's elements to "less than numerals—to buttons, clips, knobs on wheel-spokes—although one has Roman numerals."[6] In the design of the *Ball Clock*, for example, Nelson substitutes a small, round center for a traditional face; instead of pointing to numbers, slender metal hands point to round balls placed on the end of twelve metal rods. Although the Art Institute's *Ball Clock* has black fixtures and a chrome-plated center and spokes, the design was also offered in a variety of other colors and finishes.[7]

With rods and spheres that recall models of atomic structure, the *Ball Clock* helped carry this ubiquitous scientific motif into American homes. It also resembles the asterisk or starburst motifs, however, that pervaded much of

Figure 1

Advertisement for the *Storagewall*, *Architectural Forum* 81, 5 (Nov. 1944), p. 83.

Figure 2

Harry Bertoia
(American; 1915–1978).
Armchair, designed
1951/52. Made by Knoll
Associates, Incorpor-
ated, New York, N.Y.
Vinyl-covered steel
mesh, yellow naugahyde
seat pad; 77.5 x 85.7 x
71.1 cm (30½ x 33¾ x
28 in.). The Art Institute
of Chicago, gift of
Malcom, Kay, Kim, and
Kyle Kamin (1986.38).

1950s design. Like Nelson's other "Chronopak" wall clocks, it was equipped with an electric plug on the back that allowed users to move it from room to room, where it cast dramatic shadows upon the wall. While seemingly more appropriate for an office or living room, the clock most often found its way into kitchens. As Nelson explained it, the *Ball Clock* became "a sort of all-time best-seller for Howard [Miller, because] suddenly it was decided by Mrs. America that this was the clock to put in your kitchen. Why [the] kitchen, I don't know. But every ad that showed a kitchen for years after that had a ball clock in it."[8]

Like the Storagewall, Nelson designed his dramatic *Coconut Chair* to fit into an open floor plan. As he wrote in 1953, "When the walls disappear, the only place left for furniture is out in the open. Hence silhouette becomes important, and the most traditional designs for seating become unusable."[9] Indeed, the *Coconut Chair*'s sculptural form allowed owners to position it in a number of ways, and at the same time provided a bold, decorative element. Not quite organic in shape, its voluminous seat simulates the scooped-out hollow of a coconut shell; the foam-rubber upholstery is devoid of traditional tufting and provides the lean profile modern designers preferred.[10]

While the chair's triangular shell includes a continuously upholstered seat, back, and arms in the tradition of the eighteenth-century "easy" or "wing" chair, its fiberglass body and extremely thin aluminum legs clearly express the aesthetics and technology of postwar design. The rapid development of plastics during World War II provided furniture designers with yet another material to experiment with, and molded fiberglass shells, following in the tradition of the Eameses' molded-plywood furniture (cat. no. 22), became fashionable. Wartime advancements in the manufacture of bent- and welded-steel rods were also exploited by furniture designers such as Harry Bertoia (fig. 2) and Nelson, who incorporated wire and rods into their pieces; Nelson himself favored metal legs because he believed that they increased the appearance of space in an interior.[11] In his *Coconut Chair*, three anchoring legs are attached to the shell in a tripod fashion, and are further supported by thinner, interconnecting rods that lend a dynamic quality to the piece.

Like his *Ball Clock*, Nelson's *Coconut Chair* defies convention, and departs from the severe, rectilinear forms that characterized his first modular line for Herman Miller. The designs that Nelson created for the firm in the mid-to-late 1950s, including the famous *Marshmallow Sofa* (1956), suggest the beginning of a new "look" in American furniture, which, according to designer and theorist Arthur Pulos (see cat. no. 31), may be attributed to America's isolation from European design trends during World War II.[12] Indeed, Nelson's playful shapes reject historical precedent, and undoubtedly added a lighthearted element to American homes following the devastation of the war.

29. Eero Saarinen

(American, born Finland; 1910–1961)

Armchair, 1955/57

Made by Knoll Associates, Incorporated,
New York, New York
Fiberglass-reinforced plastic and lacquered
aluminum with silk upholstery; 80.7 x 65.7 x 58.4 cm
(31³/₄ x 25⁷/₈ x 23 in.)
Gift of Knoll International, 1971.15

Table, 1955/57

Made by Knoll Associates, Incorporated,
New York, New York
Cast aluminum and marble; 52.1 x 55.9 x 40.6 cm
(20¹/₂ x 22 x 16 in.)
Gift of Malcom, Kay, Kim, and Kyle Kamin, 1986.37

In his pedestal chair and table, the last of his furniture designs, Eero Saarinen attempted to eliminate what he viewed as a cluttered "slum of legs," designing instead seats and tabletops supported by a single aluminum base.[1] The culmination of several years of sketching, modeling, and full-scale experimentation, these sculptural pieces—part of the larger "Pedestal Group"—represent a significant aesthetic development, and an important technological one as well. The armchair, composed of a cast-aluminum base, fiberglass shell, and a colorfully upholstered pad of latex foam, was the result of Saarinen's unsuccessful attempt to create a strong fiberglass base that would both provide the stability of four legs and also blend with a fiberglass seat to give the appearance of a unified, organic object. Since Saarinen and the Knoll Associates' research team were unable to develop such a base due to the limited state of contemporary plastics technology, they executed the design with an aluminum base that was lacquered to match the seat's plastic finish. Although Saarinen was disappointed with this outcome, the "Pedestal Group" was a commercial success. The pieces were relatively inexpensive because they consisted of two to three component parts, and the tables and chairs inspired "lyrical comparisons to wine glasses—and even tulips."[2]

The son of Eliel Saarinen, famed Finnish architect and president of the Cranbrook Academy of Art (see cat. no. 19), Eero Saarinen immigrated to the United States with his family in 1923. He began his prolific architectural career in 1936, and, until his death in 1961, practiced a freely organic form of modernism that existed in marked contrast to the International Style that largely dominated the postwar era.[3] Saarinen was responsible for such renowned buildings as the Trans World Airlines terminal at New York's John F. Kennedy International Airport (1962), the iconic Gateway Arch in St. Louis, Missouri (1964), and residential commissions such as the Irwin Miller home (1953/57) in Columbus, Indiana.[4] Charles Eames, capturing the experimental nature of Saarinen's work, characterized his career as one of "concept and procedure, rather than form."[5] Indeed, in both his buildings and his furniture, Saarinen explored a wide variety of construction methods and industrial materials in order to create individual modern designs, which, in the case of the "Pedestal Group," featured extraordinary forms unlike anything previously produced in America.

From 1939 to 1941, Saarinen taught in the architecture department at Cranbrook, where his molded-furniture experiments with Charles Eames (see cat. no. 22) not only embodied the sort of collaborative efforts the academy encouraged, but also foreshadowed Saarinen's future achievements in fiberglass. After Eames moved to California in 1941, the two designers separately continued their crusade to develop affordable, well-designed, mass-produced furniture.

Around 1946, three years after he joined Knoll Associates as a designer, Saarinen began to experiment with shell-like seats made from molded fiberglass.[6] It was the strength of fiberglass, a glass-reinforced plastic developed for aircraft radar domes during World War II, that enabled both Saarinen and Eames to design separately a single, molded-shell seat that could be mass-produced, unlike the plywood example that they conceived together in 1940 (see cat. no. 22). In 1948, Saarinen's experiments yielded the first fiberglass chair to be mass-manufactured in the United States (fig. 1).[7] Popularly called the "Womb" Chair because of its extreme comfort, it consists of a thin, metal frame and legs that support a shell molded to the human form and upholstered with fabric-covered latex foam. By contrast, Saarinen's "Pedestal Group" leaves the fiberglass shell exposed, indicating the progress of his experiments. The lack of upholstery on the back and arms of the Art Institute's chair points to the further refinement of the durable material, which presented Saarinen with a pliable substance he could use to create the smooth, continuous, organic curves that characterize much of his work.

Figure 1

Eero Saarinen. *Armchair* (*"Womb" Chair*), 1948. Made by Knoll International, New York, N.Y. Cowhide upholstery over plastic shell; 89.2 x 55.9 cm (35⅛ x 22 in.). The Art Institute of Chicago, gift of Mrs. Albert H. Newman (1973.356).

30. Renard Koehnemann

(American; 1908–1999)

Chalices and Patens, 1955/65

Chicago, Illinois

Chalices: Silver with gold-plated bowl and black onyx; 16.5 x (diam. of bowl) 14 cm (6 1/2 x 5 1/2 in.), 2001.1.1. Silver with gold-plated bowl and red enamel; 16.5 x (diam. of bowl) 10.5 cm (6 1/2 x 4 1/8 in.), 2001.2.1. Silver with gold-plated bowl and green aventurine; 17.2 x (diam. of bowl) 11.1 cm (6 3/4 x 4 3/8 in.), 2001.3.1. Silver with gold-plated bowl and onyx; 17.8 x (diam. of bowl) 12.1 cm (7 x 4 3/4 in.), 2001.4.1.

Marked on bottom of chalices: *HAND WROUGHT/ STERLING/RAK*

Gift of Walter Placko in memory of Renard Koehnemann, 2001.1.1–2; 2001.2.1–2; 2001.3.1–2; 2001.4.1–2

The jury for the "Designer Craftsmen U.S.A., 1953" exhibition, which traveled to The Art Institute of Chicago in 1954, defined a "craftsman" as "one who creates out of basic materials, from his own design, by his own skill and the best techniques of his craft, an object which fulfills its useful purpose to the satisfaction of the user and the beholder."[1] Likewise, Chicago metalsmith Renard Koehnemann believed that a "genuine work of art" must be not only "original," but must also be designed and made by the same hand.[2] Like the Art Institute's Tiffany and Company pitcher (cat. no. 25), Koehnemann's four opulent chalices—each made with a coordinating paten—unite traditional materials and handcrafted methods with modern angles and shapes.

Raised in a devout Catholic family, Koehnemann began his studies of contemporary religious art at the College of Fine Arts at the University of Illinois in his native Champaign-Urbana. There, he quickly became immersed in the written works of the English sculptor and Catholic convert Eric Gill, who derived his theories of art from the writings of Saint Thomas Aquinas.[3] Koehnemann also studied philosophy at DePaul University in Chicago, where he continued to explore Saint Thomas's ideals of beauty—"integrity, due proportion, and resplendent form"—which he later applied to his own metalwork.[4] Soon after leaving DePaul, he became a student of Daniel Pederson of the Kalo Shop, Chicago's premier source for handwrought silver wares in the first half of the twentieth century. Pederson taught Koehnemann the fundamentals of metalworking, and undoubtedly instilled in him both Kalo's standard of excellence in workmanship, and its devotion to the belief that a true work of art must be handmade, and each piece one-of-a-kind.[5]

Many silversmiths during the 1940s and 1950s resisted machine manufacture, and, to sustain their livelihood, relied upon custom orders and commissions for sterling objects and jewelry from department stores. Presentation pieces, trophies, and wedding gifts constituted a large portion of their business. The Roman Catholic Church also served as a client, requesting handmade religious objects such as altar crosses, chalices, and monstrances. Indeed, Pope Pius XII himself confirmed the value of handmade objects in a 1947 address, stating that:

The craftsman transforms his raw material and carries through the whole of the work; and the work thus produced is intimately bound up with his own technical and artistic ability; it bears the stamp of his good taste and the marks of the finesse and dexterity of his hands. From this point of view it is far superior to the impersonal and standardized projects of the assembly line.[6]

While other Chicago metalsmiths—including those at Kalo—made ecclesiastical objects for local churches, Koehnemann devoted his entire career to such work. First, he made custom-designed wedding rings, and between 1948 and 1967, he utilized the Kalo Shop's facilities to produce approximately 270 sets of sterling-silver chalices and patens. While the chalice and paten are traditionally used in the ceremony of the Eucharist—the chalice to hold the wine and the paten for bread—Koehnemann's chalices were intended as keepsake gifts for newly ordained priests. He conceived each piece based on conversations with his clients, who were often relatives of the recipient; he then executed a drawing, and handcrafted the chalices from sheets of sixteen-gauge sterling silver.[7] The Art Institute's chalices are exceptional, in part, because the artist kept them for himself.

Koehnemann claimed that each of his chalices was unique, and although he did not repeat his designs, he did concede to "[using] some parts of one design . . . [to] design a new chalice."[8] He subscribed to the long-lived and influential Arts and Crafts notion that "the machine has no joy in its labor and none to impart to its products," and the visible hammer marks on most of his pieces, like those on the Art Institute's Tiffany pitcher, are reminiscent of Arts and Crafts metalwork.[9] As the Art Institute's chalices suggest, Koehnemann experimented with a variety of shapes, and decorated his creations with colored stones, synthetic materials, and religious symbols ranging from recognizable emblems, such as the green-aventurine Crown of Thorns and the raised Pax symbol, to inscriptions that he devised himself. The chalice with the red enamel base, for instance, proclaims: "Love One Another."

31. Arthur Pulos

(American; 1917–1997)

Beverage Server with Cover, 1956

Syracuse, New York

Sterling silver and ebony; 24.1 x 14 cm
(9½ x 5½ in.)

Stamped on bottoms of server and cover:
PULOS (in a rectangle); *STERLING*

Restricted gift of Marilyn and Thomas L. Karsten
in honor of her parents, Gertrude and Perry S.
Herst, 1985.513

William Frederick

(American; born 1921)

Teapot, 1960

Chicago, Illinois

Sterling silver and ebony; 19.7 x 23.5 cm
(7¾ x 9¼ in.)

Stamped on bottom: *HANDWROUGHT STERLING
FREDERICK*

Gift of the Antiquarian Society through the
Mrs. Myron F. Ratcliffe Fund in memory of
Myron F. Ratcliffe, 1991.108a–b

Like Oscar Riedener and Renard Koehnemann
(see cat. nos. 25 and 30), silversmiths Arthur
Pulos and William Frederick continued to
follow the Arts and Crafts–inspired tradition
of metalworking after World War II. Yet even
though such handcraft traditions remained
strong after the war, informing the work of
designers such as Maija Grotell and Gertrud
and Otto Natzler (see cat. no. 24), metalwork
such as Pulos's and Frederick's was influenced by the aesthetics of machine manufacture as well. The Art Institute's beverage
server and teapot unite traditional materials

such as sterling silver and ebony, for example, but they do not exhibit the visible hammer-marks associated with handcraft; instead, they display the smooth, undecorated metal surfaces typical of machine-produced objects, and suggest their makers' training in industrial metalwork. Furthermore, both pieces are extremely functional: reduced to bodies, lids, and handles, they possess a simplicity that resembles that of the International Style aesthetic, which was enthusiastically revived in the prosperous 1950s.[1]

After World War II, silversmiths faced a diminished market for their work, since machine-made, plated wares had become an abundant and affordable alternative to sterling silver. Furthermore, growing, busy families preferred materials that were easy to maintain, and that fit into the casual environment of new suburban homes, where fewer formal dining rooms helped foster an unceremonious style of entertaining. Craftspeople who worked in sterling silver were thus forced to rely upon private commissions, presentation pieces, and liturgical silver to support themselves. Many artists, including Pulos and Frederick, found a professional niche in university settings, which made it possible for them to "take on commissions for unique products or to indulge in the limited production of articles for sale, usually on consignment, in contemporary shops."[2]

Pulos shared the beliefs of the American Craftsmen's Council, which held that the "philosophical justification of craft" was an artist's "personal commitment to aesthetic expression."[3] Receiving a master's degree in 1941 from the University of Oregon, where he specialized in ecclesiastical silversmithing, Pulos soon contributed to the war effort by serving as head of the Aircraft Metalwork program for Air Force officers at Yale University.[4] At the end of the war Pulos traveled to Europe, where he worked on aircraft-metal maintenance, and continued to pursue his interest in handcrafted silver design by observing modern silversmiths abroad. While in Paris, for example, he visited the atelier of French silversmith Jean Puiforcat, who employed traditional smithing techniques to create simple, luxurious, modern forms that he often embellished with rare woods, semi-precious stones, and other rich materials.[5] After returning to the United States, Pulos enjoyed a long career as a teacher, designer, and theorist, during which he created jewelry, religious objects, and handmade vessels such as the Art Institute's server, and wrote several articles and books on modern American design.[6]

Pulos showed his work in a number of exhibits, including the Art Institute's "Designer Craftsmen, U.S.A., 1953," to which he contributed a cocktail pitcher and "stirring oar" (fig. 1), as well as his "Taper" flatware.[7] Executed in silver, these pieces closely resemble the jury's description of what good "Designer Craftsmen" metalwork should be. Such objects, the jury specified, should possess a design that is "refreshing in its relief from past or outside influences;" they should also "show individuality with emphasis upon form and usefulness, [and] . . . have beauty in their spirit, directness, and simplicity."[8] These standards also apply to the Art Institute's beverage server, which the United States government commissioned for the American Pavilion at the 1958 "Exposition universelle et internationale" in Brussels.[9]

Made for serving either tea or coffee, this sleek silver pot displays both directness and simplicity, and shares the functional, rational quality of Bauhaus objects such as Marianne Brandt's brass, ebony, and silver teapot (see cat. no. 10, fig. 1). The tall, slender, and slightly flattened cylindrical body of Pulos's piece is devoid of obvious hammer-marks and ornament, and flares subtly outward at the top.

Pulos sculpted both the handle and the crescent-shaped finial from rich ebony, which reveals his admiration for Puiforcat's use of splendid, contrasting materials. Both right- and left-handed servers can use the piece, since the slightly concave lid is easily reversed for pouring on either side.

Like Pulos's design, William Frederick's spare, utilitarian teapot incorporates ebony in its lid and handle, and lacks any superfluous ornament. Trained as an aeronautical engineer at both Harvard University and the Massachusetts Institute of Technology, Frederick worked as a product engineer early in his career.[10] Hoping to apply his engineering skills to handmade objects, he subsequently enrolled at The School of the Art Institute of Chicago, where he studied metalwork under silversmith Daniel Pedersen (see cat. no. 30). Frederick went on to specialize in custom presentation pieces, jewelry, and decorative pieces for churches, homes, and offices. Like Pulos, he eventually gravitated toward an academic environment, and began teaching metalworking at Chicago's Loyola University in 1974.[11]

Frederick's talent was widely celebrated in Chicago; in 1961, for example, the Art Institute exhibited his silver in a solo show entitled "Liturgical and Secular Silver by William Frederick" (see fig. 2). Although the Art Institute's teapot displays the austere, Bauhaus influences seen in Pulos's work, it also possesses a lively sense of individuality that may suggest a subtle move away from the International Style, which became increasingly outmoded in the 1960s.[12] The cantilevered finial, tapered and flared spout, and dynamic handle that hovers dramatically over this teapot's triangular body, for example, indicate Frederick's attention to distinct, creative shapes, and his skills as a designer-craftsman.

Figure 1

Arthur J. Pulos (American; 1917–1997). *Cocktail Pitcher and Stirring Oar*, c. 1953. Photo: *Designer Craftsmen U.S.A., 1953* (New York, 1953), p. 62.

Figure 2

Photograph of William Frederick featured in "Liturgical and Secular Silver" by Willam N. Frederick, The Art Institute of Chicago, April 22–June 11, 1961. Ryerson and Burnham Archives, The Art Institute of Chicago.

A Selected List of Decorative Arts Exhibitions Held at The Art Institute of Chicago, 1917–65

"Sixteenth Annual Applied Arts Exhibition"
(Oct. 9–28, 1917)
Applied Arts Exhibition: The Art Institute of Chicago Catalogue of the Sixteenth Annual Exhibition of Applied Art and Original Designs for Decorations (Chicago, 1917)

"Seventeenth Annual Applied Arts Exhibition"
(Oct. 8–27, 1918)
Applied Arts Exhibition: The Art Institute of Chicago Catalogue of the Seventeenth Annual Exhibition of Applied Art and Original Designs for Decorations (Chicago, 1918)

"Eighteenth Annual Applied Arts Exhibition"
(Oct. 7–26, 1919)
Eighteenth Annual Exhibition of Applied Arts (Chicago, 1919)

"Silverware by Georg Jensen"
(opened Jan. 14, 1921)
George Jensen: An Artist's Biography (Copenhagen, 1920)
See cat. nos. 3, 15

"Nineteenth Annual Applied Arts Exhibition and British Arts and Crafts"
(Mar. 8–Apr. 5, 1921)
Catalogue of the Nineteenth Annual Exhibition of Applied Arts and the Exhibition of British Arts and Crafts (Chicago, 1921)

"Twentieth Annual Applied Arts Exhibition"
(Sept. 22–Oct. 23, 1921)
Catalogue of the Twentieth Annual Exhibition of Applied Arts (Chicago, 1921)

"Modern Austrian Art, Assembled by Wiener Werkstätte of America"
(Sept. 19–Oct. 22, 1922)
See Barter, fig. 1

"Twenty-First Annual Applied Arts Exhibition with the Association of Arts and Industry"
(May 1–31, 1923)
Catalogue of the Twenty-First Annual Exhibition of Applied Arts (Chicago, 1923)
See cat. no. 1

"Twenty-Second Annual Applied Arts Exhibition with the Association of Arts and Industry"
(May 1–June 1, 1924)

"Twenty-Third Annual Arts and Crafts Exhibition"
(Dec. 23, 1924–Jan. 25, 1925)
Catalogue of the Twenty-Third Annual Exhibition of Modern Decorative Art at the Art Institute of Chicago (Chicago, 1925)
See cat. nos. 1, 3, 5, 10

"International Exposition of Modern Decorative Arts"
(May 3–30, 1926)
A Select Collection of Objects from the International Exposition of Modern Decorative & Industrial Art at Paris, 1925 (Chicago, 1926).
See p. 20

"Swedish Contemporary Decorative Arts"
(Aug. 9–Oct. 14, 1927)
Exhibition of Swedish Contemporary Art (Chicago, 1927)
See Barter, fig. 8

"International Exhibition of Contemporary Metalwork and Cotton Textiles"
(Jan. 19–Mar. 1, 1931)
Decorative Metalwork and Cotton Textiles: Third International Exhibition of Contemporary Industrial Art (Portland, Maine, 1930)
See cat. nos. 6, 13

"Peasant Art of Sweden and Norway"
(June 1–Nov. 1, 1934)
Peasant Art: Sweden, Norway: A Century of Progress Exhibition (Chicago, 1934)

"Swedish Tercentenary Art Exhibit, Lent by the Swedish Government"
(Feb. 4–Mar. 6, 1938)
Swedish Tercentenary Art Exhibit (Stockholm, 1937)

"Steuben Glass"
(Feb. 11–Mar. 24, 1938)
Exhibition of Steuben Glass: The Art Institute of Chicago (Chicago, 1938).
See cat. no. 17

"Architecture by Mies van der Rohe"
(Dec. 15, 1938–Jan. 15, 1939)

"Contemporary Ceramics of the Western Hemisphere"
(Jan. 22–Feb. 23, 1942)
Contemporary Ceramics of the Western Hemisphere (Syracuse, 1942)
See cat. no. 24

"Modern Art Becomes Advertising: Advertising Designs for the Container Corporation of America"
(Apr. 28–June 24, 1945)
Modern Art in Advertising: an Exhibition of Designs for Container Corporation of America (Chicago, 1945)
See Barter, n. 24

"Modern Ceramics and Woodenware"
(Mar. 1–Apr. 30, 1946)
See p. 88

"Designer Craftsmen, U.S.A., 1953"
(Mar. 16–Apr. 26, 1954)
Designer Craftsmen, U.S.A, 1953 (New York, 1953)
See cat. nos. 24, 30, 31; p. 73, fig. 3

"Midwest Designer-Craftsmen, 1957"
(Mar. 27–Apr. 24, 1957)
Midwest Designer-Craftsmen: Exhibition of Works by Designer-Craftsmen of the Mississippi Basin (Chicago, 1957)

"Pottery by Toshiko Takaezu"
(through Nov. 20, 1960)
See cat. no. 24

"Liturgical and Secular Silver by William N. Frederick"
(Apr. 22–June 11, 1961)
See p. 103, fig. 2

"Ceramics by Gertrud and Otto Natzler"
(Apr. 13–June 9, 1963)
Ceramics by Gertrud and Otto Natzler (Chicago, 1963)
See cat. no. 31

Notes

Editor's note: For the specific dates of Art Institute exhibitions, please consult the "Selected List of Decorative Arts Exhibitions held at The Art Institute of Chicago, 1917–65," on p. 104 of this publication.

Recommended Reading

The following publications offer a further introduction to twentieth-century American decorative arts. For ease of reference, they receive short citations within the notes.

Cheney and Candler Cheney 1936. Sheldon Cheney and Martha Candler Cheney, *Art and the Machine: An Account of Industrial Design in 20th-Century America* (New York/ London, 1936).

Clark 1983. Robert Judson Clark et al., *Design in America : The Cranbrook Vision, 1925–1950,* exh. cat. (New York/ Detroit, 1983).

Darling 1984. Sharon Darling, *Chicago Furniture, 1833–1983: Art, Craft & Industry,* (Chicago/ New York, 1984).

Davies 1983. Karen Davies, *At Home in Manhattan: Modern Decorative Arts, 1925 to the Depression,* exh. cat. (New Haven, 1983).

Hiesinger and Marcus 1993. Kathryn B. Hiesinger and George H. Marcus, *Landmarks of Twentieth-Century Design: An Illustrated Handbook* (New York, 1993).

Hine 1986. Thomas Hine, *Populuxe.* (New York, 1986).

Johnson 2000. J. Stewart Johnson, *American Modern, 1925–1945: Design for a New Age,* exh. cat. (New York, 2000).

Kardon 1995. Janet Kardon, ed., *Craft in the Machine Age: The History of Twentieth-Century American Craft, 1920–1945,* exh. cat. (New York, 1995).

Kirkham 2000. Pat Kirkham, ed., *Women Designers in the USA, 1900–2000: Diversity and Difference,* exh. cat. (New York, 2000).

Miller 1990. R. Craig Miller, *Modern Design in the Metropolitan Museum of Art* (New York, 1990).

Neuhart et al. 1989. John Neuhart, Marilyn Neuhart, and Ray Eames, *Eames Design: The Work of the Office of Charles and Ray Eames* (New York, 1989).

Pulos 1988. Arthur Pulos, *The American Design Adventure: 1940–1975* (Cambridge, Mass., 1988).

Wilson 1986. Richard Guy Wilson et al., *The Machine Age in America, 1918–1941,* exh. cat (New York, 1986).

BARTER, "Designing for Democracy: Modernism and Its Utopias," pp. 6–17

1. Walter Gropius, "Program of the Staatliche Bauhaus in Weimar," in Hans M. Wingler, *The Bauhaus: Weimar, Dessau, Berlin, Chicago* (Cambridge, Mass., 1969), p. 31. Frank Caspers, "Patrons at a Profit—Business Discovers Art as a Selling Force," *Art Digest* 17,15 (May 1, 1943), p. 5. Leszek Kolakowski quoted in Hilton Kramer, "Abstraction & Utopia, II: From Theosophy to Utopia," *New Criterion* 16, 1 (Sept. 1997), p. 12.
2. Raymond Williams, *The Politics of Modernism: Against the New Conformists* (New York, 1989), p. 43.
3. See Members of the Institute of Design/ Illinois Institute of Technology, "Manifesto, 1955," in Wingler (note 1), p. 214.
4. For a social history of the Arts and Crafts movement and its impact in America, see T. J. Jackson Lears, *No Place of Grace: Antimodernism and the Transformation of American Culture, 1880–1920* (New York, 1981).
5. The Art Institute sponsored Arts and Crafts exhibitions beginning after the English designer Charles Robert Ashbee's trip to Chicago in 1898. Ashbee's Guild of Handicraft, a communal association of craftspersons based on medieval models, inspired Clara Barke Wells to form the Kalo silversmith's community in suburban Park Ridge, Illinois. For more on the Boston Society of Arts and Crafts, see Wendy Kaplan et al., *"The Art That is Life": The Arts & Crafts Movement in America, 1875–1920,* exh. cat. (Boston, 1987), pp. 299–300.
6. William Morris, quoted in Gillian Naylor, ed., *William Morris by Himself: Designs and Writings* (London, 1988), p. 212.
7. For more on this theme, see Howard Mansfield, *Restoration and Renewal in a Throwaway Age* (Hanover, N. H., 2001).
8. See Johnson 2000, pp. 14–16.

9. Gabriel Mourey, "L'Art nouveau de M. Bing à l'Exposition universelle," *Revue des Arts Décoratifs* 20 (1900), p. 280. See also Debora Silverman, *Art Nouveau in Fin-de-Siècle France: Politics, Psychology, and Style* (Berkeley, 1989).
10. Nancy J. Troy, *Modernism and the Decorative Arts in France: Art Nouveau to Le Corbusier* (New Haven, 1991), p. 50.
11. At the 1925 Paris exposition, modernists such as Le Corbusier, who embraced a reformist philosophy and designed versatile furnishings incorporating new technology, competed uneasily with traditional French designers, for whom decoration was distinct from integrated architectural or design elements. See ibid., pp. 160–69.
12. Herbert Hoover, then U.S. Secretary of Commerce, quoted in International Exposition of Modern Decorative and Industrial Art, Paris, *Report of Commission* (Washington, D.C., 1925), p. 16.
13. William M. R. French, quoted in Barry Shifman, "Design for Industry: The 'German Applied Arts' Exhibition in the United States, 1912–13," *The Decorative Arts Society 1850 to the Present* vol. 22 (1998), p. 25. The exhibition's American tour was organized by John Cotton Dana, Librarian of the Newark Free Public Library, Newark, N.J., in collaboration with the Deutscher Werkbund and the Deutsches Museum für Kunst in Handel und Gewerbe, Hagen. The exhibition appeared in Chicago from Aug. 10–Sept. 16, 1912.
14. William Laurel Harris, "Back to Duncan Phyfe—or Forward to Art Nouveau?," *Good Furniture Magazine* 19, 6 (Dec. 1922), p. 259.
15. The Metropolitan Museum of Art, New York, also hosted this exhibition in 1927.
16. Miller 1990, p. 18.
17. "Modern Decorative Art in Chicago," *Good Furniture Magazine* 30, 2 (Feb. 1928), pp. 72–73.
18. Darling 1984, pp. 273–74. See also *Good Furniture Magazine* (note 17), pp. 72–74.
19. The Association of Arts and Industries and the Art Director's Club of Chicago both helped organize this exhibition, which featured furniture crafted from exotic woods, Rodier upholstery, and decorative accessories by René Lalique. The exhibition opened in October 1928. See "Modern Rooms in New York and Chicago," *Good Furniture Magazine* 31, 6 (Dec. 1928), pp. 315–16.
20. "On Exhibition in Chicago Stores," *Good Furniture and Decoration* 33, 5 (Nov. 1929), pp. 269–74.
21. Athena Robbins, "Distinctive Rooms at Marshall Field's," *Good Furniture Magazine* 32, 6 (June 1929), p. 325.
22. Miller (note 16), p. 27.
23. Barbara Hauss-Fitton, "Streamlining at the World's Fair: Chicago 1933/34–New York 1939/40," in Claude Lichtenstein and Franz Engler, eds., *Streamlined: A Metaphor for Progress: The Esthetics of Minimized Drag,* exh. cat. (Baden, 1995) pp. 68–75.
24. Chicago, the heart of the nation's mail-order advertising and printing business during the 1920s and 1930s, was a logical place for modernist graphic design to flourish. Paepcke, along with the architectural firm of Skidmore, Owings and Merrill, was instrumental in bringing modernists (specifically Moholy and Mies) to the New Bauhaus in Chicago. The Art Institute hosted an exhibition of the Container Corporation of America's innovative graphic designs, entitled "Modern Art Becomes Advertising." For more on Paepcke, see James Sloan Allen, *The Romance of Commerce and Culture: Capitalism, Modernism, and the Chicago-Aspen Crusade for Cultural Reform* (Chicago, 1983).
25. Abbott Laboratories, DeBeers, *Life* and *Fortune* magazines, and Pan American Airlines all employed modernist designs in their advertising efforts. For more on modernism and the corporation, see Judith A. Barter, "The New Medici: Corporate Collecting and Uses of Contemporary Art" (Ph.D. diss., University of Massachusetts at Amherst, 1991).
26. Wright, quoted in "Snapshots: Russel and Mary Wright," *Interiors* 104, 5 (Dec. 1944), p. 86. Departing from the streamlined aesthetic, organic modernist design relied on smoother, curvilinear forms, and incorporated traditional materials such as ceramics, fabrics, and wood.
27. For more on the American middle class in the 1950s, see Loren Baritz, *The Good Life: The Meaning of Success for the American Middle Class,* (New York, 1990), pp. 182–201.
28. William Morris, quoted in Naylor (note 6), p. 224.

DOWNS, "The New Modern Feeling": A Catalogue of the Collection

"The Modern Spirit," pp. 19–21

1. Paul T. Frankl, *New Dimensions* (New York, 1928), p. 20.
2. Rena Rosenthal, for example, opened a shop in New York City where she sold modern Austrian objects as early as 1916. See Diane H. Pilgrim, "Design for the Machine Age," in Wilson 1986, p. 277.
3. In 1913, Elsie de Wolfe published an extremely influential decorating guide that promoted eighteenth-century French- and English-style furnishings. Although she encouraged her readers to buy bona-fide antiques, she also endorsed historically accurate reproductions. Elsie de Wolfe, *The House in Good Taste* (New York, 1913), pp. 261–64.
4. *Report of Commission Appointed by the Secretary of Commerce to Visit and Report upon the International Exposition of Modern Decorative and Industrial Arts in Paris, 1925,* quoted in Johnson 2000, p. 8.

5. Johnson 2000, p. 15. For an illustration of Le Corbusier's "Pavilion," see ibid., p. 15.
6. Here, visitors saw Danish porcelains, French furniture, Danish silver, and Swedish glass, among other objects. For illustrations of this exhibition as shown at The Metropolitan Museum of Art, New York, see Nellie C. Sanford, "The Loan Exhibition from the Paris Exhibition shown in the Metropolitan Museum of Art," *Good Furniture Magazine* 26 (Apr. 1926), pp. 185–88. The exhibition also traveled to Boston, Cleveland, Detroit, St. Louis, Minneapolis, Pittsburgh, and Philadelphia.
7. Pilgrim (note 2), p. 292.
8. Dr. Wilhelm Lotz, "German Furniture of the Twentieth Century," *Good Furniture Magazine* 31 (Nov. 1928), p. 238.
9. Frankl (note 1), p. 76.
10. Paul T. Frankl, "Just What is this Modernistic Movement?" *Arts & Decoration* 28, 1 (May 1928), p. 67.

1. Henry Varnum Poor, pp. 22–23

1. The show was intended to "[encourage] men and women with artistic gifts to produce designs which would lift the manufactures on a large scale from the commonplace to the very desirable." See "Beauty in Crafts at Art Institute," *Chicago Post*, May 8, 1923, n.p. From "Scrapbook of The Art Institute of Chicago," Ryerson Library, hereafter referred to as AIC Scrapbook. For prizewinning entries, see "Applied Arts Prizes," in *Chicago Evening Post*, May 22, 1923, n.p. (AIC Scrapbook). For more general information on this exhibit, see *Catalogue of the Twenty-First Annual Exhibition of Applied Arts*, exh. cat. (Chicago, 1923).
2. Helen Comstock, "A Painter Who Became a Potter," *International Studio* 79, 324 (May 1924), p. 136.
3. Harold E. Dickson et al., *Henry Varnum Poor, 1887–1970: A Retrospective Exhibition*, exh. cat. (University Park, Penn., 1983), p. 39.
4. Henry Varnum Poor, *A Book of Pottery: From Mud to Immortality* (Englewood Cliffs, N. J., 1958), pp. 42–43.
5. Davies 1983, p. 46. Poor not only succeeded as a painter and a potter, but he also worked as a designer of furniture and interiors. He participated in a number of exhibitions, including the 1928 and 1929 American Designers' Gallery shows. For more on these exhibitions, see cat. no. 10.
6. Comstock (note 2), p. 136.
7. Henry Varnum Poor, quoted in Dickson et al. (note 3), p. 41. Poor's exhibition, entitled "Decorated Pottery, Paintings, and Drawings by H. Varnum Poor," took place at the Montross Gallery, New York, in 1923.

2. William Hunt Diederich, pp.23–25

1. Quoted in F. Newlin Price, "Diederich's Adventure in Art," *International Studio* 81, 337 (June 1925), p. 171.
2. Mrs. Gordon-Stables, "Old English Firebacks," *International Studio* 81, 336 (May 1925), pp. 129–32. In some of the early reviews of Diederich's firescreens, mention was always made of the practical use of these works, and of how the artist employed fire, in a sense, as a compositional element.
3. "Art in France," *Burlington Magazine* 24, 3 (Dec. 1913), p. 172.
4. Guy Pène du Bois, "Hunt Diederich, Decorator, Humorist and Stylist," *Arts and Decoration* 7, 11 (Sept. 1917), p. 515.
5. The lamp bracket is illustrated in ibid., p. 516; the sculpture appears in an unidentified newsclipping preserved in the Archives of American Art, Smithsonian Institution, roll 3950, frame 152.
6. Janis C. Conner and Joel Rosenkranz, "Hunt Diederich," in *Rediscoveries in American Sculpture: Studio Works, 1893–1939* (Austin, Tex., 1989), p. 22. For most of the designs that the Art Metal and Iron Company fabricated for Diederich, see Hunt Diederich Papers, Archives of American Art, Smithsonian Institution, roll 3339, frame 146.
7. Charles Fabens Kelley, "Hunt Diederich," *Chicago Tribune*, Nov. 4, 1934, n.p.
8. See The Art Institute of Chicago, *Catalogue of the Twenty-Third Annual Exhibition of Modern Decorative Art at The Art Institute of Chicago*, exh. cat. (Chicago, 1924).
9. John Shapley, like other critics in the 1920s, also remarked on this aspect of Diederich's work: "Diederich, essentially a modern, nevertheless keeps a leg over the stile and trifles with the very near past." John Shapley, "Art Activities in New York," *Parnassus* 1, 4 (Apr. 1929), p. 5.
10. Christian Brinton, "Hunt Diederich," in *Catalogue of the First American Exhibition of Sculpture by Hunt Diederich*, exh. cat. (New York, 1920), n.p.
11. In particular see Conner and Rosenkranz (note 6), pp. 19–26.

3. Erik Magnussen, pp. 26–27

1. "Modern Silver Design: Erik Magnussen Leads a Trend Toward Plainer Patterns," *Good Furniture Magazine* 26 (June 1926), p. 291. For information about Magnussen's career after Gorham, see Tara Lee Tappert, "Resource List," in Kardon 1995, pp. 239–40. For more on Magnussen's work for Gorham, consult Charles H. Carpenter, Jr., *Gorham Silver, 1831–1981* (New York, 1982), pp. 257–64.

2. Helen Appleton Read, "Twentieth-Century Decoration: A Modern Theme Finds a Distinctive Medium in American Silver," *Vogue* 72, 1 (July 1, 1928), p. 58.
3. Ibid.
4. Davies 1983, p. 20.
5. In addition to his covered cups, Magnussen also designed a conservative, less expensive line of spun and stamped silver called "The Modern American." See Gorham Manufacturing Company, *The Modern American* (New York, 1928), n.p., mentioned in Charles Venable, *Silver in America, 1840–1940: A Century of Splendor*, exh. cat. (Dallas, 1994), p. 280.
6. William Codman, *An Illustrated History of Silverware Design* (Providence, R.I., 1930), p. 72.

4. Adelaide Alsop Robineau, pp. 27–29

1. See Alice Cooney Frelinghuysen, "Aesthetic Forms in Ceramics and Glass," in Doreen Bolger Burke, ed., *In Pursuit of Beauty: Americans and the Aesthetic Movement*, exh. cat. (New York, 1986) pp. 220–29. For more on the Atlan Ceramic Club, see Sharon Darling, *Chicago Ceramics and Glass*, exh. cat. (Chicago, 1979), pp. 17–27.
2. For more on Robineau, see Alice Cooney Frelinghuysen, *American Porcelain: 1770–1920*, exh. cat. (New York, 1989), pp. 61–64, 276–79, 284–87, 292–301.
3. For more on Binns and the American studio ceramic movement, see Margaret Carney, *Charles Fergus Binns: The Father of American Studio Ceramics*, exh. cat (New York, 1998).
4. See Frelinghuysen (note 2), p. 64.
5. Robineau produced the *Scarab Vase*, also known as *The Apotheosis of the Toiler*, under Doat's direction. For a color illustration, see Barbara Perry, ed., *American Ceramics: The Collection of Everson Museum of Art* (New York, 1989), p. 99.
6. Barbara Hall, "Conservation Report," May 6, 1999, Files of the Department of American Arts, The Art Institute of Chicago.
7. Quoted in Frelinghuysen (note 2), p. 294.

5. Paul T. Frankl, pp. 30–32

1. "American Modernist Furniture Inspired by Sky-Scraper Architecture," *Good Furniture Magazine* 29, 3 (Sept. 1927), p. 119.
2. Paul T. Frankl, *New Dimensions: The Decorative Arts of Today in Words and Pictures* (New York, 1928), p. 19.
3. I would like to thank Christopher Long, Assistant Professor for Architectural History and Theory, University of Texas at Austin, for this information.
4. In order to provide ample light and air for both buildings and pedestrians, in 1916 New York City instituted strict building codes that required roof setbacks when a building reached a certain height. See Davies 1983, p. 64.
5. *Good Furniture Magazine* (note 1).
6. Frankl Galleries, *Skyscraper Furniture*, sales cat. (New York, c. 1928), p. 12.
7. Mary Fanton Roberts, "Modernistic Movement in Arts and Crafts," *Arts and Decoration* 28, 6 (Apr. 1928), p. 60.
8. Frankl asserted that his use of black lacquer was a modern adaptation of an "ancient craft" perfected by Chinese and Japanese craftsmen. See Paul T. Frankl, "Why we Accept Modernistic Furniture," *Arts and Decoration* 29, 2 (June 1928), p. 99.
9. See Frankl Galleries (note 6), pp. 3, 5, 7.
10. Helen Appleton Read, "Shopping for the Modern House," *Vogue* 73, 1 (Mar. 16, 1929), p. 98. See also "Modernism Reaches the Mantel," *House and Garden* 55, 3 (Mar. 1929), p. 100.
11. Read (note 10), p. 61.
12. Paul T. Frankl, *Machine-Made Leisure* (New York, 1932), p. 140.

6. Eugene Schoen, pp. 32–34

1. Ella Burns Myers, "Trends in Decoration," *Good Furniture Magazine* 31, 3 (Sept. 1928), p. 128.
2. Nellie C. Sanford, "An Architect-Designer of Modern Furniture," *Good Furniture Magazine* 30, 5 (May 1928), pp. 116–17.
3. Besides the Art Institute's cabinet, a desk is the only other piece of furniture from this suite that has come to light. This desk is now in a private collection. Author's conversation with Daniel Morris, Historical Design, Incorporated, New York, Nov. 20, 2000.
4. See Eugene Schoen, "The Design of Modern Interiors," in *Creative Art* 2, 5 (May 1928), p. 40.
5. See Howell S. Cresswell, "The Paris Exposition of Modern Decorative Arts," in *Good Furniture Magazine* 25, 4 (Oct. 1925), pp. 187–99; and idem, "The Paris Exposition of Modern Decorative Arts, Continued," in *Good Furniture Magazine* 25, 6 (Dec. 1925), p. 317.
6. One example of such an exhibition is R. H. Macy and Company's "International Exposition of Art in Industry" in 1928, where Schoen displayed a model living room; see R. H. Macy and Company, *An International Exposition of Art in Industry*, exh.

cat. (New York, 1928), p. 68. A few years later, the designer presented a circular aluminum table with a Bakelite® top at the "International Exhibition of Decorative Metalwork and Cotton Textiles," organized by the American Federation of Arts. See the American Federation of Arts, *Catalogue of the International Exhibition of Decorative Metalwork and Cotton Textiles*, exh. cat. (New York, 1930), where Schoen's table appears as cat. no. 412.

7. One of Schoen's most important domestic commissions was the home of Morris and Gwendolyn Cafritz, prominent residents of Washington, D.C. Schoen planned the interiors and furnishings for the Cafritz residence, which was designed by architects Alvin Aubinoe and Harry Edwards and completed in 1937. I would like to thank Eric Koehler for this information.

8. Sanford (note 2), pp. 116–18.

7. Donald Deskey, pp. 34–36

1. David A. Hanks and Jennifer Toher, "Donald Deskey's Decorative Designs," *The Magazine Antiques* 131, 4 (Apr. 1987), p. 843.
2. For illustrations of the store windows and a screen, see David A. Hanks with Jennifer Toher, *Donald Deskey: Decorative Designs and Interiors* (New York, 1987), pp. 12–17, 35.
3. For illustrations of the Gimbel and Rockefeller apartments, see ibid., pp. 76–77, 79, 80–83.
4. For more on his 1928 entry, the "Man's Smoking Room," see Mary Fanton Roberts, "Beauty Combined with Convenience in Some Modernistic Rooms," *Arts and Decoration* 30, 4 (Feb. 1929), p. 112, ill. Deskey designed a living room for the Second Annual Designers' Gallery exhibition. See Shepard Vogelgesang, "Contemporary Interior Design Advances," *Good Furniture Magazine* 32, 5 (May 1929), p. 230, ill. For other illustrations of the "Man's Smoking Room" and the "Living Room," see Hanks (note 2), pp. 22–24.
5. For an illustration of this early Ypsilanti tubular-steel furniture, see Hanks and Toher (note 1), pp. 842–43.
6. This "Vitreo" metal top was offered alongside a "veneer" version; see Ypsilanti Reed Furniture Company, *Reed and Fibre Furniture*, sales cat. (Ionia, Mich.; c. 1929), n.p. I would like to thank Daniel Morris, Historical Design, Incorporated, New York, for this source.
7. Donald Deskey, "The Rise of American Architecture and Design," *London Studio* 5, 2 (Apr. 1933), p. 238.
8. John Gloag, "Wood or Metal," *Creative Art* 4, 1 (Jan. 1929), p. 50.

8. Reuben Haley, pp. 37–38

1. Shirley Paine, "Shop Windows of Mayfair," *Garden and Home Builder* 47 (July 1929), p. 510. Also quoted in Wilson 1986, p. 294.
2. *Crockery and Glass Journal* 106 (May 1928), p. 35.
3. See Jack D. Wilson, *Phoenix & Consolidated Art Glass, 1926–1980* (Marietta, Oh., 1989), p. 40–55.
4. Kopp Glass, Incorporated, of Swissvale, Penn., also produced a line of "Modernistic" glassware resembling "Ruba Rombic." In an attempt to discourage such competitors, Consolidated patented several of its "Ruba Rombic" designs; Haley received a patent for a vase similar to the Art Institute's on Feb. 1, 1928 (serial no. 25127).
5. For prices, see *Crockery and Glass Journal* (note 2), p. 83. "Special gift numbers," presumably targeted at retailers, were advertised at inexpensive prices. See "Ruba Rombic Special Gift Numbers," *The Gift and Art Shop* (Dec., 1928), p. 78.
6. *Crockery and Glass Journal* (note 2), p. 83.

9. Gene Theobald, pp. 39–40

1. International Silver Company, "New Sophistication in Keeping with Fine Old Traditions of Silversmithing," advertisement in *House and Garden* 55, 5 (May 1929), p. 149.
2. Davies 1983, pp. 66–67.
3. International Silver Company (note 1).
4. In 1928, International Silver also produced a line of modern silver tableware called "Spirit of Today," designed by Alfred G. Kintz. See Davies 1983, p. 96.
5. Douglas Haskell, "A Fine Industrial Design," *Creative Art* 3, 6 (Dec. 1928), pp. l–li.
6. *Creative Art* 4, 1 (Jan. 1929), p. 22; quoted in Davies 1983, p. 76. Silverplating, or electroplating, is a process by which a coating of silver is electrolytically deposited on a less expensive base metal.
7. Cited in Davies 1983, p. 96.
8. International Silver Company (note 1), p. 149.
9. For more on the hand finishing of these objects, see Alistair Duncan, *Modernism: Modern Design 1880–1940: The Norwest Collection: Norwest Corporation, Minneapolis* (Woodbridge, Suffolk, U.K, 1998), p. 226. For the quote, see *Creative Art*

(note 6), p. 51.

10. Ilonka Karasz, pp. 41–42

1. For an illustration of these companion pieces, see Helen Sprackling, "Modern Art and the Artist," *House Beautiful* 65, 2 (Feb. 1929), p. 153.
2. Harry V. Anderson, "Contemporary American Designers," in *Decorator's Digest* 5 (Dec. 1935), pp. 46–47.
3. Between 1925 and 1973, for example, Karasz designed 186 cover illustrations for the *New Yorker*. For more on Karasz's life and work in various media, see Ashley Brown, "Ilonka Karasz: Rediscovering a Modernist Pioneer," in *Studies in the Decorative Arts* 8,1 (fall/winter 2000–2001), pp. 69–91.
4. Karasz displayed batiks and a decorated box at this exhibition. See The Art Institute of Chicago, *Catalogue of the Twenty-Third Annual Exhibition of Modern Decorative Art at The Art Institute of Chicago* (Chicago, 1924), cat. nos. 55–56.
5. R. H. Macy and Company, *An International Exposition of Art in Industry*, exh. cat. (New York, 1928), p. 67. Although it is not listed in the catalogue, Karasz also provided a footed bowl similar to the Art Institute's for Lescaze's display. I would like to thank Ashley Brown, Curator, Henry D. Green Center for the Study of the Decorative Arts, Georgia Museum of Art, for this information.
6. The American Designers' Gallery consisted of a fifteen-member group of architects and designers that also included Raymond Hood, Ely Jacques Kahn, Winold Reiss, Herman Rosse, Martha Ryther, and Carolyn Simonson. Other designers, such as Hunt Diederich and Paul T. Frankl, participated as well. See Helen Appleton Read, "Twentieth-Century Decoration: The American Designers' Gallery, a Symposium of Modern American Decorative Art," *Vogue* 73, 1 (Jan. 19, 1929), p. 77.
7. For more on the 1928 nursery and studio apartment, see Brown (note 3), pp. 79–80.
8. Additional examples are featured in Paul T. Frankl, *Form and Re-form: A Practical Handbook of Modern Interiors* (New York, 1930), p. 10. Furthermore, the collection of The Metropolitan Museum of Art, New York, includes a bowl identical to the Art Institute's, as well as one slightly larger; see Johnson 2000, p. 121, ill. For a detailed description of Karasz's dining room, see Shepard Vogelgesang, "Contemporary Interior Design Advances," *Good Furniture Magazine* 32, 5 (May 1929), pp. 229–34.
9. C. Adolph Glassgold, "The Decorative Arts," *The Arts* 15, 4 (Apr. 1929), pp. 271–72.
10. Ibid., p. 269.
11. Jewel Stern, "Striking the Modern Note in Metal," in Kardon 1995, p. 122.

11. Kem Weber, pp. 43–45

1. From "New York—The Nation's Style Pulse," *Retailing* 1 (Apr. 13, 1929), p. 17, quoted in Davies 1983, p. 12. In 1928, for example, critic Ella Burns Meyers declared that "the modern movement in decoration is not confined or even led by Manhattan. Long before New York was speaking above a whisper about Modernism, Barker Brothers of Los Angeles were featuring the modern creations of Kem Weber." See Ella Burns Myers, "Trends in Decoration," *Good Furniture Magazine* 31, 3 (Sept. 1928), p. 128.
2. Cheney and Candler Cheney 1936, p. 56.
3. Nathan George Horwitt, "Reasoned Design," *Creative Art* 8, 5 (May 1931), p. 377.
4. David Gebhard, "Kem Weber: Modern Design in California, 1920–1940," *Journal of Decorative and Propaganda Arts 1875–1945*, 2 (summer/ fall 1986), p. 22.
5. For more on Weber's biography and a timeline of his work, see David Gebhard and Harriette Von Breton, *Kem Weber: The Moderne in Southern California 1920 through 1941*, exh. cat. (Santa Barbara, Calif., 1969).
6. "Modern Furniture from Los Angeles: Barker Bros. Feature Kem Weber's Designs," *Good Furniture Magazine* 29, 5 (Nov. 1927), pp. 233–36.
7. Ibid., p. 236.
8. Ibid., p. 235.
9. Ibid., p. 233.
10. Although Weber officially resigned as Art Director at Barker Brothers, he continued to work for the firm as a consultant.
11. See R. H. Macy and Company, *An International Exposition of Art in Industry*, exh. cat. (New York, 1928), pp. 66–67.
12. AUDAC, founded in 1928, organized two exhibitions: the first, held in 1930 at the New York Grand Central Palace, was entitled "Home Show"; the second, "Modern Industrial and Decorative Art," was held in 1931 at the Brooklyn Museum. The group also published a book in 1930, *Modern American Design*, which was reprinted as the *Annual of American Design 1931* (New York, 1930). Weber wrote a section called "The Modern Shop" in this book, which also features chapters on modern architecture, decorative arts, graphic arts, industrial design, and other design topics. See also Johnson 2000, pp. 18–21.
13. For more on the Grand Rapids Chair Company, see Christian G. Carron, *Grand Rapids Furniture: The Story of America's Furniture City* (Traverse City, Mich., 1998), pp. 153–54. The remainder of this suite is dispersed as follows: one armchair and the

sideboard in The Metropolitan Museum of Art, New York; one armchair and the dining table in the Wolfsonian-Florida International University, Miami Beach; one chair in the Denver Art Museum; one chair in the Brooklyn Museum of Art; and one armchair in a private collection.

14. The color names "Sage Green" and "Coral Red" were used to describe elements of Weber's furniture in I. B. Gorham, "Comfort, Convenience, Colour: Examples from the Designs of Kem Weber on the Pacific Coast," *Creative Art* 7, 4 (Oct. 1930), p. 252. This suite's color scheme was undoubtedly influenced by the work of Bruno Paul, who exhibited a "much admired green and silver dining room ensemble" at the 1928 R. H. Macy and Company exposition (note 11). See N. C. Sanford, "Decorating in Art Moderne: The Evidence Shows that it is Gaining in Public Favor," *Good Furniture Magazine* 31, 5 (Nov. 1928), p. 242.

15. In the 1930s, Weber designed several examples of streamlined furniture, including tubular-steel models made by the Lloyd Manufacturing Company of Menominee, Mich., as well as his famous cantilevered-plywood "Airline" chair of 1934. For illustrations of these pieces, see Gebhard and Von Breton (note 5), pp. 80–83.

"Modern Solutions," pp. 47–49

1. Donald Deskey, "The Rise of American Architecture and Design," *London Studio* 5, 25 (Apr. 1933), p. 268.
2. Jeffrey L. Meikle, *Twentieth-Century Limited: Industrial Design in America, 1925–1939* (Philadelphia, 1979), p. 29.
3. Johnson 2000, p. 34.
4. Hiesinger and Marcus 1993, p. 114.
5. For more on the exposition's model homes, see Dorothy Raley, ed., *A Century of Progress: Homes and Furnishings* (Chicago, 1934).
6. John Gloag, "Wood or Metal," *Creative Art* 4, 1 (Jan. 1929), p. 50.
7. Hiesinger and Marcus 1993, p. 76.
8. Eugene Schoen, "Industrial Design: A New Profession," *Magazine of Art* 31, 8 (Aug. 1938), p. 472.
9. "Bauhaus Exhibition," *Bulletin of the Museum of Modern Art* 5, 6 (Dec. 1938), n. p.
10. Cheney and Candler Cheney 1936, p. 193.
11. Eliot F. Noyes, *Organic Design in Home Furnishings*, exh. cat. (New York, 1941), n.p.
12. Hiesinger and Marcus 1993, pp. 117–18. For a photograph of the Pavilion, see ibid., p. 119.

12. Warren McArthur, pp. 50–51

1. Marcel Breuer, for example, designed his tubular-steel "Wassily" chair in 1925, and Ludwig Mies van der Rohe's cantilevered bent-steel chair appeared in 1927; both pieces were machine made.
2. Warren McArthur Corporation sales catalogue (Rome, New York, c. 1935), p. 69. This catalogue illustrates a number of chairs, desks, lamps, sofas, and tables, all produced using McArthur's interchangeable aluminum-tubing structure. I would like to thank Professor Pat Kirkham, the Bard Graduate Center for Studies in the Decorative Arts, New York; Denise Marchand, Director, Stuart Parr Gallery, New York; and Warren McArthur III, MACs DESIGNs, Phoenix, for this reference.
3. Avis Berman suggested that McArthur succeeded in California, despite the Depression, due to the steady work provided by the motion-picture industry. He sold his designs to film studios such as Columbia, Metro-Goldwyn-Mayer, Paramount, and Warner Brothers, and also established a prominent clientele that included several movie stars. See Avis Berman, "McArthur Returns," *Art and Antiques* 20, 10 (Nov. 1997), p. 76.
4. Many urban beauty salons received modern renovations in the 1930s. For more information on this trend, see "Beauty Salons," *Architectural Forum* 64, 5 (May 1936), pp. 407–12. I would like to thank Pat Kirkham (note 2) for this information.
5. For Warren McArthur III's recollections of his father's experiments with metal, see Berman (note 3), p. 76.
6. Warren McArthur Corporation (note 2), p. 1.
7. Ibid., p. 69.
8. The Warren McArthur Corporation label on the underside of the seat states: "This article contains/ALL NEW MATERIAL/ consisting of Kapok." Kapok is a light fiber obtained from the seed-pods of the kapok tree, and used to fill seat cushions. The label also lists the style number as "1111," the order number as "4277," and the color name as "Green Clayton."
9. Mineral dyes allowed McArthur to offer his metal designs in black, blue, bronze, gold, green, orange, red, and yellow. "Style 1111" is not on the company's 1940 price list, which suggests that by that point it was no longer available. Since the label on the underside of the seat lists the place of manufacture as Rome, N.Y., the Art Institute's chair must have been made before 1937–38, when the Warren McArthur Corporation moved to Bantam, Conn. Letter from Warren McArthur, III, to the author, Oct. 19, 2000, Files of the Department of American Arts, The Art Institute of Chicago.

13. Wolfgang Hoffmann, pp. 52–53

1. For a color illustration of a combination cigarette and match holder with ashtray, see Johnson 2000, p. 117. For more on Pola Hoffmann, see Mary Schoeser and Whitney Blausen, "Wellpaying Self Support," in Kirkham 2000, pp. 149, 151.
2. N. C. Sanford, "Modern Art Designed in America," *Good Furniture Magazine* 32, 4 (Apr. 1929), p. 186.
3. See Darling 1984, p. 314. For an illustration of Howell furniture in the U.S. Steel Building, see ibid., p. 313.
4. Howell Company, *Modern Chromsteel Furniture Catalogue #18* (St. Charles, Ill., 1937), p. 2. This catalogue is accompanied by an inclusive, unpaginated price list. For more on the model residences, see Dorothy Raley, ed., *A Century of Progress: Homes and Furnishings* (Chicago, 1934). Howell moved its factory to St. Charles, Ill., in 1936.
5. Darling 1984, pp. 312–13. For an illustration of one of Howell's tubular-metal armchairs after a design by Mies van der Rohe, see ibid., p. 313.
6. Ibid., p. 314. For illustrations of the "Lumber Industries House," see Raley (note 4), pp. 80–88.
7. During World War II, Howell's factory was converted for wartime production, and Hoffmann left the company to pursue a career in photography. See Darling 1984, p. 316.
8. Formica® (patented in 1922) is used to make laminated-plastic products such as tabletops, and is produced by infusing special papers with synthetic resins that are then exposed to heat and pressure. For more on Formica®, Fabrikoid®, and other modern materials, see Johnson 2000, p. 183. In a 1937 catalogue, Howell offered the round table with either twenty-four or thirty- inch plate glass tops, priced at $26.00 and $26.50, respectively. See Howell Company (note 4), p. 31, and price list.
9. Paul T. Frankl, "Why We Accept Modernistic Furniture," *Arts & Decoration* 29, 2 (June 1928), p. 59. For more on cocktail accessories, see Wilson 1986, pp. 328–29.
10. Howell Company (note 4), price list.
11. Ibid., p. 2.
12. Cheney and Candler Cheney 1936, pp. 182, 184. Along with Hoffmann, the Cheneys also singled out the work of Donald Deskey (see cat. no. 7), Kem Weber (see cat. no. 11), and Russel Wright (see cat. no. 16), among others.

14. Frank Lloyd Wright, Richard Neutra, pp. 54–56

1. While Wright's greatest works are well known, Neutra's most renowned buildings are less so. They include the Los Angeles Garden Apartments (1927), and the Lovell House (Los Angeles, 1929). For an introduction to Wright's work, see William Allin Storrer, *The Architecture of Frank Lloyd Wright: A Complete Catalog* (Cambridge, Mass., 1978); for more on Neutra, consult Arthur Drexler and Thomas S. Hines, *The Architecture of Richard Neutra: From International Style to California Modern*, exh. cat. (New York, 1982).
2. For illustrations of this chair design in Neutra's home/studio, known as the VDL Research House, see Henry Robert Harrison, "Richard J. Neutra, a Center of Architectural Stimulation," *Pencil Points* 18 (July 1937), p. 416; for a photo of the chair in the Catalina Island Ticket Office, see Thomas S. Hines, *Richard Neutra and the Search for Modern Architecture* (New York, 1982), p. 164. The steel-spring support was applied on at least two of Neutra's chair designs; see ibid., pp. 121–22, ill. The Art Institute's chair was made for Herschel Elarth, who worked under Neutra from 1936 to 1937. Before his death in 1988, Elarth lived in Blacksburg, Virginia, as a retired architect and Professor Emeritus of Architecture at Virginia Polytechnic Institute and State University.
3. Frank Lloyd Wright, "In the Cause of Architecture," in Frederick Gutheim, ed., *Frank Lloyd Wright on Architecture: Selected Writings, 1894–1940* (New York, 1941), p. 42.
4. Wright, quoted in Alan Crawford, "Ten Letters from Frank Lloyd Wright to Charles Robert Ashbee," *Architectural History* 131 (1970), p. 64. Wright also espoused his beliefs in an address entitled "The Art and Craft of the Machine," which he presented to the Chicago Arts and Crafts Society on Mar. 1, 1901, and published in the *Catalogue of the Fourteenth Annual Exhibition of the Chicago Architectural Club* (Chicago, 1901). The date of the lecture was erroneously published in this book as March 6. See Judith A. Barter, "The Prairie School and Decorative Arts at The Art Institute of Chicago," *The Art Institute of Chicago Museum Studies* 21, 2 (1995), p. 185, n. 40.
5. For illustrations and information on other Wright furniture in the Art Institute's collection, see Barter (note 4), pp. 126–33.
6. Wright's designs for the desk and chair are illustrated in *Architectural Forum* 68, 1 (Jan. 1938), p. 87.
7. For information on subcontractors, see Christian G. Carron, *Grand Rapids Furniture: The Story of America's Furniture City* (Traverse City, Mich., 1998), p. 213.
8. For more on the Larkin Building, including illustrations of its work spaces, see Jack Quinan, *Frank Lloyd Wright's Larkin Building: Myth and Fact* (Cambridge, Mass., 1987).

9. Jonathan Lipman, *Frank Lloyd Wright and the Johnson Wax Buildings* (New York, 1986), p. 88.
10. Although the Art Institute's chair is not one-of-a-kind, it was not mass-produced either. Neutra apparently contracted with an unknown manufacturer who used pre-fabricated metal pieces to assemble the furniture, often by hand. Herschel Elarth, "Reflections on the Era of the 1930s, Architecturally Speaking," Oct. 26, 1987, Files of the Department of American Arts, The Art Institute of Chicago.
11. Museum of Modern Art, New York, *Modern Architecture: International Exhibition*, exh. cat. (New York, 1932), p. 158.
12. Ibid., p. 16.
13. For more illustrations, see Hiesinger and Marcus 1993, p. 106.
14. Neutra included chairs with wooden frames in his Tremaine House (Montecito, Calif., 1948); for an illustration, see Hines (note 2), p. 214. The upholstery on the Art Institute's chair is not original; Mr. Elarth maintained that the original upholstery was a red-brown fabric; thus, the current upholstery is sympathetic to the original. See Herschel Elarth to Milo Naeve, Sept. 4, 1987, Files of the Department of American Arts, The Art Institute of Chicago. Contemporary photographs indicate that the chair was offered in fabric or vinyl upholstery. See Harrison (note 2), p. 416.

15. Peer Smed, pp. 57–58

1. Earl Chapin May, *Century of Silver 1847–1947: Connecticut Yankees and a Noble Metal* (New York, 1947), p. 277.
2. Jewel Stern, "Striking the Modern Note in Metal," in Kardon 1995, p. 128.
3. May (note 1), p. 277. Smed collaborated with Frederick Stark, a designer for the International Silver Company (see cat. no. 9) on designs for the Waldorf Astoria hotel's flatware and holloware services; see Stern (note 2). Smed also made copper busts, illustrated in Samuel Howe, "Sculptor as Metal Worker: The Hammered Copper Statues of Peer Smed," *Arts & Decoration* 3, 12 (Oct. 1913), pp. 404–405. An owl-shaped cocktail shaker (1931; 1990.179), and a silver pin (1930/39; 1989.69), both designed by Smed, are also in the Art Institute's collection.
4. See Smed's obituary, *New York Times*, Nov. 20, 1943, p. L-13.
5. For more on the silver designs of Jensen and other Danish craftsmen, see Janet Drucker, *Georg Jensen: A Tradition of Splendid Silver* (Atglen, Penn., 1997); and David Revere McFadden, ed., *Scandinavian Modern Design, 1880–1980*, exh. cat. (New York, 1982).
6. A number of Danish silversmiths, including Jensen and Michelsen, exhibited work at the "International Exhibition of Contemporary Metalwork and Cotton Textiles." For a list of venues, exhibitors, and dates, see *Decorative Metalwork and Cotton Textiles: Third International Exhibition of Contemporary Industrial Art*, exh. cat. (Portland, Maine, 1930).
7. Stern (note 2), p. 122.
8. Elizabeth MacRae Boykin, "Modern Silver Put on Display: Metropolitan Museum has Contemporary Showing," *New York Sun*, Apr. 10, 1937, p. 10.

16. Russel Wright, pp. 59–61

1. For more on Wright's philosophy of informal decoration, see "Snapshots: Russel and Mary Wright," *Interiors* 104, 5 (Dec. 1944), p. 86. I would like to thank Suzanne Lampert, formerly Curatorial Documentation Assistant in the Department of American Arts, for her research and written contributions to this catalogue entry.
2. Hiesinger and Marcus 1993, p. 399.
3. Quoted from *Interiors* (note 1). For example, Wright created the "Modern Living" (later called "American Modern") and "Blonde Modern" furniture lines for the Conant Ball Company of Gardner, Mass., in 1935 and 1936, respectively. For a list of Wright's manufactured designs, see William J. Hennessey, *Russel Wright: American Designer* (Cambridge, Mass., 1983), pp. 91–93.
4. In 1921 Wright entered Princeton University, where he became involved in theatrical design. Between 1916 and 1927, Norman Bel Geddes designed many stage productions; after 1927, he turned his attention to the streamlined consumer products for which he is best known. His "Oriole" gas stove of 1931–36, for example, revolutionized kitchen-range design; for an illustration, see Hiesinger and Marcus 1993, p. 130.
5. For more on Wright's early consulting work, see ibid., pp. 27–35.
6. Ann Kerr, *The Collector's Encyclopedia of Russel Wright Designs* (Paducah, Ky., 1990), p. 70. This publication lists the many different forms included in the "Oceana" line.
7. For more on Wright's "American Way" line, see Hennessey (note 3), pp. 47–51. In addition to the "Oceana" box, the Art Institute's holdings of "American Way" designs also include a wrought-iron chair (1942) by Henry Glass (2000.132; see cat. no. 26).
8. "Notes on the Exhibition of Useful Objects," *Bulletin of The Museum of Modern Art* 6, 6 (Jan. 1940), pp. 3, 5–6.
9. Charles Venable et al., *China and Glass in America 1880–1980: From Tabletop to TV Tray*, exh. cat. (Dallas, 2000), p. 349; p. 72, color ill.
10. For a list of color options, see Hennessey (note 3), p. 89, n. 19.

11. Lecock and Company of New York, N.Y., produced the table linens; John Hull Cutlery manufactured the flatware; and the Morgantown Glass Guild of Morgantown, W.V., was responsible for the glassware.
12. Iroquois China Company of Syracuse, N.Y., manufactured "Casual China" and Northern Industry Chemical of Boston, Mass., executed "Residential" and "Flair." During the 1950s and 60s, Wright continued to design furniture, tableware, textiles, and small appliances; for a list of these objects, see Hennessey (note 3), pp. 91–93. Wright also engaged in public speaking and participated in exhibitions; between 1950 and 1955, for example, he regularly displayed his work at the "Good Design" shows organized for the Museum of Modern Art, New York, and the Merchandise Mart, Chicago.

17. Sidney B. Waugh, Paul Manship, pp. 62–65

1. For more on Gates and Waugh, see Mary Jean Madigan, *Steuben Glass: An American Tradition in Crystal* (New York, 1982), pp. 65–75.
2. Steuben Glass, Incorporated, *Steuben Glass, with an Introduction by Sidney Waugh* (New York, 1947), p. 8.
3. These pieces of Swedish glass—the bottle (fig. 1), a vase (1925.47), and an unidentified object—were purchased from the Atlan Club Fund at the "Twenty Third Annual Arts and Crafts Exhibition" in 1924–25. For more on these and other purchases from this exhibition, see The Art Institute of Chicago, *Bulletin of The Art Institute of Chicago* 19, 2 (Feb. 1925), pp. 21–23.
4. This exhibition was held at The Metropolitan Museum of Art, New York, from Jan. 18 to Mar. 20, 1927. Designed by Carl G. Bersten, the architect for the Swedish Pavilion at the 1925 Paris exposition, the installations included glass pieces made by Kosta and Orrefors. See The Art Institute of Chicago, *Exhibition of Swedish Contemporary Art*, exh. cat. (1927), p. 8. For more on Swedish Glass, see Anne-Marie Ericsson et al., *The Brilliance of Swedish Glass 1918–1939: An Alliance of Art and Industry*, exh. cat. (New Haven, 1996).
5. Derek E. Ostergard, "Modern Swedish Glass in America, 1924–1939," in Ericsson et al. (note 4), p. 139.
6. The New York show took place at the M. Knoedler and Company gallery, and included fifteen pieces of the new Steuben glass; at least twenty examples of this colorless glass were exhibited at the Fine Art Society in London. See The Fine Art Society, *Exhibition of Steuben Glass*, exh. cat. (London, 1935), p. 5.
7. Ibid, p. 14.
8. For an illustration of this piece, see Ericsson et al. (note 4), p. 147.
9. The Art Institute of Chicago, *Exhibition of Steuben Glass: The Art Institute of Chicago*, exh. cat. (Chicago, 1938), n.p.
10. See *Chicago Daily News*, Feb. 17, 1938, n.p. (AIC Scrapbook). The Art Institute also purchased Waugh's *Pegasus Vase* (1938.216) from the exhibition.
11. Madigan (note 1), p. 93.
12. See Steuben Glass, Incorporated, *Collection of Designs in Glass by Twenty-Seven Contemporary Artists*, exh. cat. (New York, 1940), cat. no. 20. Manship's design drawings for the vase's decorative scheme are in the collection of the Minnesota Museum of Art, St. Paul; for more information and illustrations, see Minnesota Museum of Art, *Paul Manship: Changing Taste in America*, exh. cat. (St. Paul, 1984), cat. nos. 91–93.
13. Manship had already pursued his fascination with ancient Greece through bronze sculptures such as *Centaur and Dryad* (1913; New York, The Metropolitan Museum of Art), and the *Infant Hercules* fountain, made for the courtyard of the American Academy in Rome. For a discussion of Manship's classical design sources and their relationship to modernism, see Susan Rather, "The Past Made Modern: Archaism in American Sculpture," *Arts Magazine* 59, 3 (Nov. 1984), pp. 111–19. For an illustration of *Centaur and Dryad*, see ibid., p. 114.

18. Margret Craver, pp. 66–67

1. Jeannine Falino, "Women Metalsmiths," in Kirkham 2000, p. 232.
2. Among Craver's other teachers during the 1930s were Wilson Weir of Tiffany and Company in New York, and Leonard Heinrich, Chief Armor Conservator at The Metropolitan Museum of Art, New York. She also studied at the studio of the Stone Associates in Gardner, Mass. See National Women's Caucus for Art, *Honor Awards for Outstanding Achievement in the Visual Arts* (San Francisco, 1989), p. 1.; and Jeannine Falino, "MFA Boston acquires Craver Silver Teapot," *Antiques and The Arts Weekly*, Feb. 16, 1990, p. 50.
3. Fleming's work was exhibited at the Art Institute in 1931, when the museum hosted the "International Exhibition of Metalwork and Cotton Textiles," and was also displayed at Chicago's 1933 "Century of Progress International Exposition." For more on Fleming and for illustrated examples of his work, see Jan von Gerber, *Erik Fleming—Atelier Borgila* (Stockholm, 1994), p. 76.
4. Kirk, for example, made a silver hand-mirror with an enamel medallion in colors similar to those on the Art Institute's bonnbonnière; see J. David Farmer, "Metalwork and Bookbinding," in Clark 1983, p. 151, color ill.

5. Elizabeth Moses, quoted in *Decorative Arts: Official Catalog, Department of Fine Art, Division of Decorative Arts, Golden Gate International Exposition San Francisco*, exh. cat. (San Francisco, 1939), p. 81. In Craver's possession until the Art Institute purchased it in 1985, the bonbonnière won an award from the Philadelphia Art Alliance in 1938.

6. For more regarding Craver's association with Handy and Harman, see Tara Lee Tappert, "Resource List," in Kardon 1995, p. 232.

19. J. Robert F. Swanson, Pipsan Saarinen Swanson, and Eliel Saarinen, pp. 67–69

1. I would like to thank Mark Coir, Director, Cranbrook Archives, Bloomfield Hills, Mich., for this information. Coir also suggested that "*FHA* had an additional advantage in that all the pieces were proportional to one another and could therefore easily be laid out on a grid, making it possible for amateurs to easily conceptualize furniture placement in rooms." Mark Coir to the author, Feb. 14, 2001, Files of the Department of American Arts, The Art Institute of Chicago.

2. For more on Saarinen's architecture, interiors, and applied arts designs, see Clark 1983.

3. In 1923, Saarinen and his family immigrated to Evanston, Ill., after he was awarded second prize in the international competition for the Chicago Tribune Tower.

4. The interior decoration of Cranbrook's buildings was a result of an intense family collaboration: Saarinen's wife Loja designed many of the textiles; and daughter Pipsan and son Eero (see cat. no. 29) conceived furnishings and decorative elements. See Ashley Brown, *Backgrounds for Modern Living: Furniture, Textile and Fashion Designs by Pipsan Saarinen Swanson*, exh. cat. (Bloomfield Hills, Mich., 1999), n.p.

5. Pipsan Saarinen Swanson to Ann Stacy, Executive Director, Michigan Society of Architects, July 29, 1969, J. Robert F. Swanson and Pipsan Saarinen Swanson Papers, Cranbrook Archives, Bloomfield Hills, Mich. Quoted in Brown (note 4), n. 10. For more on the Swanson-Saarinen partnerships, see Johnson 2000, p. 181.

6. The Swansons and Saarinen were also undoubtedly familiar with Aalto's "Finnish Pavilion" at the 1939 World's Fair in New York, which was exhibited the same year that the *FHA* line was first produced.

7. See the promotional brochure *F.H.A.: Flexible Home Arrangements* (New York, c. 1940), n.p., Cranbrook Archives, Bloomfield Hills, Mich. For color illustrations of the nesting tables with a stainless-steel top, see Johnson 2000, p. 163.

"The Shapes of Progress," pp. 71–73

1. T. H. Robsjohn-Gibbings, *Goodbye Mr. Chippendale* (New York, 1944), p. 4.

2. Hiesinger and Marcus 1993, p. 152.

3. "American Industrial Design," *Bulletin of the Museum of Modern Art* 8, 1 (Nov. 1940), p. 11.

4. "International Competition for Low-Cost Furniture Design," *Bulletin of The Museum of Modern Art* 15, 2 (Jan. 1948), p. 13.

5. Arthur Pulos, *The American Design Adventure: 1940–1975* (Cambridge, Mass., 1988), p. 86.

6. Ibid., p. 110.

7. "Good Design," *American Artist* 16, 3 (Mar. 1952), p. 70.

8. The Museum of Modern Art, New York, *Good Design: An Exhibition of Home Furnishings Selected by The Museum of Modern Art, New York, for the Merchandise Mart, Chicago* (New York, 1953), inside cover; quoted in Hiesinger and Marcus 1993, p. 177.

9. *Interiors* 117, 2 (Sept. 1957), p. 134. "Modern Museum's Choice," *The Art Digest* 27 (Oct. 15, 1952), p. 22.

10. Hiesinger and Marcus 1993, p. 179.

11. Thomas Hines, *Populuxe* (New York, 1986), p. 38.

20. Samuel A. Marx, pp. 74–76

1. The Blocks donated a number of nineteenth- and twentieth-century paintings to The Art Institute of Chicago; for more on their art collection, see The National Gallery of Art, Washington, D.C., *100 European Paintings and Drawings from the Collection of Mr. and Mrs. Leigh B. Block*, exh. cat. (Washington, D.C., 1967). The Art Institute's collection includes five additional pieces of furniture that Marx designed for the Block apartment around 1944: a plywood-and-tupelo table (1981.173); a maple, magnolia, yellow poplar, and hardwood-veneer table (1981.175); a birch-and-parchment table (1981.176); and two birch, hardwood-veneer, and plastic side chairs (1981.177–78). For illustrations, see Eileen and Richard Dubrow, *Styles of American Furniture: 1860–1960* (Atglen, Penn., 1997), pp. 167, 169, 170.

2. Samuel Marx and his wife, Florene May Schoenborn Marx, collected Native American pottery, eighteenth-century English furniture, modern French paintings, and contemporary Swedish rugs. For more on their collection of paintings, see the Museum of Modern Art, New York, *The School of Paris: Paintings from the Florene May Schoenborn and Samuel A. Marx Collection*, exh. cat. (New York, 1965). The Marxes gave a number of artworks to the Art Institute, where Samuel served as a trustee from 1952 to 1962, and an Honorary Trustee from 1962 until his death in 1964.

3. Robsjohn-Gibbings designed several pieces of furniture with forms and ornament inspired by Greek and Roman prototypes. See Rosemarie Haag Bletter, "The World of Tomorrow: The Future with a Past," in Lisa Phillips et al., *High Styles: Twentieth-Century American Design*, exh. cat. (New York, 1985), pp. 111–12.

4. See Carlos A. Rosas, "Modern Custom Furniture: Unique Pieces from Mid-century Commissions," *Architectural Digest* 53, 8 (August 1996), pp. 30–32.

5. Darling 1984, p. 285.

6. See Athena Robbins, "Decorating the Business Office: Lending Character and Efficiency to Commercial Surroundings," *Good Furniture Magazine* 31, 3 (Sept. 1928), pp. 134–35. The author praised Marx for his modern entrance lobby and private office, which "combine colonial and modernistic elements."

7. "The Pump Room," *Architectural Forum* 73, 1 (July 1940), p. 21.

8. "Noted Architect Samuel A. Marx Dies at 78," *Chicago Sun-Times*, Jan. 18, 1964, p. 12.

9. "Meet Samuel Marx," *House Beautiful* 87, 11 (Nov. 1945), p. 120. Quoted in Darling 1984, p. 284.

10. Darling 1984, p. 284. Marx's furniture strongly resembles that of the French designer Jean-Michel Frank; see Galerie Jacques de Vos, *Jean–Michel Frank, Adolphe Chanaux: "Intérieurs,"* exh. cat. (Paris, 1990).

11. "Furniture that Starts as Architecture: Grounded in the Past . . . but Appreciative of the Future," *House Beautiful* 90, 10 (Oct. 1948), p. 148.

12. Liz O'Brien, *Samuel Marx: Furniture and Decoration*, exh. cat. (New York, 1996), pp. 8–9.

13. Marion Gough, "How to Develop an Appreciation of Art," *House Beautiful* 89, 3 (Mar. 1947), p. 144.

14. Ibid., p. 82. The location of the second table is unknown.

15. Marx achieved this effect by applying multiple layers of different-colored paints and then heat-baking the finish until the top coat split into an allover network of cracks. See *House Beautiful* (note 11).

16. Marx seems to have produced several chairs in this design, including one for his own apartment at 1325 Astor Street in Chicago. For photographs of this apartment, see "Connoisseur's Modern: S. A. Marx Apartment, Chicago," *House and Garden* 79, 4 (Apr. 1941), pp. 34–37. Marx's own chair was identical in design, yet featured dark legs and a light-colored seat, back, and arms.

21. Edward Wormley, pp. 77–78

1. Dunbar Furniture Corporation, *Dunbar Book of Modern Furniture* (Berne, Ind., 1953), p. 7. For more on Wormley's biography and early career, see Judith B. Gura, Chris Kennedy, and Larry Weinberg, eds., *Edward Wormley: The Other Face of Modernism*, exh. cat. (New York, 1997), pp. 2–8.

2. "Janus House" advertisement, *Interior Design* 28, 9 (Sept. 1957), p. 136.

3. "Edward Wormley: A Quarter Century of Design," *Interior Design* 27, 5 (May 1956), p. 94.

4. Ibid, p. 120.

5. *Interior Design* (note 3).

6. Dunbar Furniture Corporation, press release, (Berne, Ind., c. 1951), Trade Literature Collection, Cooper-Hewitt National Design Museum, Smithsonian Institution.

7. Judith B. Gura, "Rediscovering Wormley: The Late Dunbar Designer is Gaining a New Following," *Interior Design* 68, 2 (Feb. 1997), p. 22.

8. The mate resides in a private collection.

9. Gura, Kennedy, and Weinberg (note 1), p. 10.

10. "Career Group" advertisement, *Interior Design* 24, 10 (Oct. 1953), p. 19. The cushion is not original to the bench, but was made from a Wormley-designed textile known as "Brenta" (c. 1950).

22. Charles and Ray Eames, pp. 79–82

1. The Art Institute's collection of the Eameses' work also includes an *LTR* (Low Table [with] Rod [base]) (1950; 1977.179); a wire-mesh chair (1951/53; 1976.395); a molded-fiberglass rocking chair (1950/53; 1976.396); and a teak-and-leather sofa (prototype 1967, produced 1984; 1984.398). For more on the Eameses' work, see Neuhart et al. 1989.

2. Charles was trained as an architect at Washington University in St. Louis, where he subsequently founded several different firms, including Gray & Eames (1930), and Eames & Walsh (1935). After graduating from high school in 1931, Ray Kaiser began a career as a graphic designer and a painter; in 1933 she studied under the painter Hans Hoffmann in New York.

3. For more on their career and collaboration, see Neuhart et al. 1989, and Pat Kirkham, *Charles and Ray Eames: Designers of the Twentieth Century* (Cambridge, Mass., 1995), pp. 61–95.

4. Neuhart et al. 1989, p. 25. For illustrations of the Eames and Saarinen prototypes, see Eliot F. Noyes, *Organic Design in Home Furnishings*, exh. cat. (New York, 1941), pp. 10–17.

5. For an illustration of the "Kazam!" machine and a molded prototype seat, see Neuhart et al. 1989, p. 27.

6. For more on the Eameses' designs for the war effort, and for illustrations of their